"As a warrior, I found *We Also Serve: A Family Goes to War* to be a gripping, unforgettable story of a military family's emotional survival through two wars. With humility, compassion, and courage Nanette writes as the wife and the mother of combat Marines—through the full range of PTSD, anger, drugs, and marriage difficulties—while chronicling a spirit of survival. The legacy of freedom continues when their Marine son deploys to Iraq, with the result that the ownership of PTSD now extends from father and mother to a son and his family. *We Also Serve: A Family Goes to War* will set a fire in your heart."…

Colonel Billy R. (Bill) Duncan, USMC, Ret. Commanding Officer of 2nd Battalion, 1st Marines in Vietnam in 1968.

Bill Duncan ("Texas Pete - 6") grew up in Texas in the shadow of WW II. His heroes were family, friends and a nation that embraced patriotism. The defining thirty-one years of his life were those in the Marine Corps, in which he served in over eighty countries including combat tours in Korea—receiving a battlefield commission as a second lieutenant. Besides being 2/1's commanding officer in Vietnam, he served in Borneo, Malaysia, Southeast Asia, Africa, and the Middle East with the British Royal Marines. He was a Distinguished Graduate (1974/5) of the National War College and was appointed Executive Director of the Marine Corps Amphibious Warfare Team. He served as the G-3 Operations Officer for the 3rd Marine Division and Amphibious Forces in 1977/8 (covering the area from Alaska in the north to Australia in the south). Retired as a colonel, he remains faithful to his Enlisted and Officers Oaths of Service to America. "So help me God."

WE ALSO SERVE

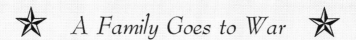

★ *A Family Goes to War* ★

Nanette Sagastume

iUniverse, Inc.
Bloomington

We Also Serve
A Family Goes to War

iUniverse books may be ordered through booksellers or by contacting:

iUniverse
1663 Liberty Drive
Bloomington, IN 47403
www.iuniverse.com
1-800-Authors (1-800-288-4677)

ISBN: 978-1-4620-3089-7 (sc)
ISBN: 978-1-4620-3091-0 (hc)
ISBN: 978-1-4620-3090-3 (e)

Printed in the United States of America

iUniverse rev. date: 4/16/2012

For my husband and my son, with love and
gratitude for their service to our country

Those also serve who only stand and wait.

—John Milton (1608-1674),
Sonnet XIX: When I Consider How My Light is Spent, Line 14

Contents

Acknowledgments

I would have been unable to write this book without the active support and encouragement of my husband, Mario. He believed enough in the value of my story, particularly as it pertains to PTSD, and was humble enough to permit me—even encourage me—to tell my stories despite the fact that many were unflattering to him. I respect him for his service to our country as a Marine in Vietnam—despite not being a U.S. citizen at the time. And I am grateful for his love and friendship over the decades as well as his companionship as we coped with having a son in combat.

I am enormously grateful to Daniel, who has allowed me to tell the story of the Labor Day bombing. I have agreed to state that he does this with hesitation and discomfort. This event feels private to him because it is, after all, *his* story and these are *his* friends. Yet, I was so affected by these events that his story became part of my story too. We both have concerns that the details, even without identifying the victims, may be too raw for the families of those killed. I do not wish to cause these families additional anguish. I have tried to strike a balance between being too reserved and too boldly descriptive of that scene. But I needed to include the description in order to illustrate why my reaction was so profound. If I have added to the pain of any of the families, I am deeply sorry.

I am humbled by the courage Daniel has displayed, not only in the course of his combat deployment, but also in revisiting these events as he reviewed the manuscript for me for its accuracy.

As for the rest of my children, I think they have been perplexed by my project and probably have doubted it would ever come to fruition.

Nonetheless, I am indebted to them for their honesty and courage in allowing my words to stand publicly if, by doing so, it can benefit other families.

Of course, I must acknowledge my friends in the Chico Military Family Support Group—especially Cheryl, Chris, Dan, Desi, Debbie, Sue S., and Theresa—who have inspired and encouraged me, my friend Janet who urged me to start the support group in the first place, as well as my friend and co-worker Kathy, Sue P., and the many others who lent their ears when I verbalized my fears.

The families of those who served in 2/1 in Iraq with my son Daniel—and who comprised my online family—and of course my husband's Marine brothers, the Vietnam Veterans of 2/1, are very much a part of my story. They offered their love, support, and prayers; we could not have gotten through Daniel's deployment without them.

I am honored to know Colonel Billy R. Duncan, who commanded 2nd Battalion 1st Marines in 1968 (after Mario had left Vietnam). He is the dignified embodiment of an officer and a gentleman, who, even in retirement, still watches over his Marines.

I am eternally grateful to Dr. Judy Brislain and Dr. Aldrich "Pat" Patterson, who steered our family over the years through the eddies of our lives. In no small measure, our family is intact to this day because of their love and skill in helping us build on the positives of our relationships. Having helped us through the rough waters of these military years, both of these counselors have enthusiastically encouraged me to publish my story.

Gratitude is owed to Elizabeth Evans, for helping me through these faith-challenging years.

Though my Operation Homecoming essay did not appear in the anthology of the same name, I am grateful to Jon Peede and Andrew Carroll for the opportunity to express myself, which, in turn, provided the initial inspiration for me to write my story. I am gratified that my essay was posted on the Operation Homecoming Web site.

I am especially indebted to my freelance editor Suzanne Byerley, of Choice Words, for helping me condense the original, unwieldy manuscript without changing its tone or intent. When the task seemed too overwhelming, she offered direction and encouragement.

I can't write a book about the military experience without offering an earnest thank you to those men and women, who volunteer to guard and defend us, and to their families. We Americans owe so much to you; we can never repay your generosity. God bless you.

Introduction

When our son Daniel left in June 2001 for Marine Corps boot camp, the World Trade Center's twin towers still pierced the New York skyline. Americans bustled about their business, complacent in the belief that their country was impervious to harm. Four days after my son's graduation from boot camp, when the Towers crumbled, so did my world, as I realized that Daniel would now go to war.

War had already woven itself into the family's emotional tapestry as a result of my husband Mario's combat service with the Marine Corps in Vietnam. When Daniel became part of the War on Terror, war would once again shape our family. By virtue of technological advances in the past several decades—live video news feeds, e-mails, satellite phones, webcams, Skype—families have become inadvertent real-time companions to their warriors on the battlefield.

On November 10, 2009, Mario and I and hundreds of Marine veterans attended ceremonies at the Marine Corps War Memorial, where the keynote speaker was the former Chairman of the Joint Chiefs of Staff, retired Marine General Peter Pace. My heart lifted to hear him tip his hat to the often-overlooked role of military families. Scribbling quickly to pen his words that morning, I wrote:

"Our military families have served our country as well as anyone who has worn the uniform of the United States. When we Marines are tired, our families dust us off, tell us they love us, and send us back. And when we come back from war, our families stand in the background while we get our decorations and medals."

My story traces how my husband's and my son's military services affected—indeed altered—our family's relationships in ways that surprised and, sometimes, dismayed us.

Mario's combat service had been an intermittent leitmotif in the years of our early marriage as he began to experience the after-effects of war. The emotional roller coaster of Daniel's military service began with his Marine boot camp graduation, but continued even after his return to civilian life. Not only the warriors, but family members, too, may suffer combat-related Post-Traumatic Stress.

The morning of September 7, 2001, pride washed over me as I watched the new Marines graduate from boot camp. More than five hundred young men, fiercely proud, their right hands angled crisply in rigid salutes, stood in precise columns before a crowd of beaming families and friends. Though puffed with maternal pride, I gradually became aware of a darker emotion below the surface, one that mystified me, even as it vaguely disquieted me. What was wrong, I wondered, just before awareness bore down on me: these new Marines had just offered to put their lives down for us. The significance of that gift pierced me. Their youthfulness prevented them from appreciating the magnitude of their commitment. Even though our country was not at war, I knew peace could never be guaranteed.

With the events of 9/11, the next four years challenged my views about the world, patriotism, non-violence, the morality of war, and the will of God. Our relationships with many family and friends were fractured over the politics of war. I have yet to resolve questions of the morality of war in general—this war in particular—however, further internal debate was a luxury my heart could not afford while my son was in harm's way. If my son's morale was key to his well-being, I could not risk anything that might damage it.

Despite the terrible anxiety triggered in me as well as the fractured relationships provoked by passions about the war, living in constant tension provided an exhilarating edge. My life was more desperate, yet more intense and focused. All my emotions seemed sharper even though they were much more mercurial than at any other time in my life. There was an intoxicating sense of immediacy, of dealing with what was purest and most fundamental in life.

Then, too, there was the thrill of my association, even if vicarious, with events shaping history. While it is true that these years were fraught with angst, they were also heady times.

Daniel's boot camp graduation turned out to be one of several events during his service that jarred my world and forever changed me. I didn't foresee that his decision to serve would have such a profound impact on my life. But how could I have imagined the world itself would shift a mere four days after his graduation?

Knowing how polarizing different perspectives on the war's merits can be, I do not wish my story to be construed as for or against the war. Rather, I believe the military family's story is too important to risk it being dismissed for reasons of politics. With one percent of Americans volunteering to serve, there is a gap in awareness—even a "disconnect"—about the military family's experience. Instead, I ask the reader to accompany me, as I relate how our family served, and continues to serve, our country.

Prologue

Labor Day 2004
7 AM, September 6

The morning was already too oppressively hot for me to sleep any later. I eased myself out of bed and padded barefoot toward the kitchen. Mario was already up, watching the television news channel. We planned a relaxed Labor Day morning before attending the memorial service for a local Marine, killed in Iraq, whom we did not know but wished to honor.

As I pressed the start button on the coffeemaker, Mario recounted a dream that left him unsettled.

His gaze drifted as he recalled, "You know me—I usually can't remember my dreams. But this one is different somehow. In any of the dreams I've ever had about Daniel, he is always a little kid, no more than two or three years old, sitting on my lap. What's strange about this dream is that he was the age he is now.

"As I walk down the hallway from our bedroom, Daniel comes from the opposite direction. He's wearing those tan cargo pants and the light blue shirt that he likes to wear—you know the ones. In real life I always give him a hug, right? Well, in my dream, I reach out to give him a hug and to kiss him on the neck, and, for some reason, we both start to cry.

"But the weirdest part? Even though I was dreaming, I could actually *smell* him! His scent was real; it was like Daniel was here. I woke up at that point, but the dream is still so vivid that I can't get it out of my mind. It's like he was really here."

I pondered Mario's dream as I poured my coffee. Mug in hand, I moved to the adjacent room to scan our desktop computer, eagerly checking for any overnight e-mails from Daniel, but there were none.

Mario sipped his coffee in the family room, leisurely watching the television news. As I answered e-mail correspondence, I half-listened to the commentator. My attention was suddenly riveted by the news that, during our nighttime, a suicide bomber in the Fallujah area had crashed into a military convoy, killing seven Marines.

Instantly Mario and I looked apprehensively at each other across the expanse of two rooms. "Shit!" he exploded.

I vainly attempted to push down my rising anxiety. I scolded myself: Now, Nanette, there are hundreds of 2/1 Marines based in Fallujah and hundreds more Marines from other battalions scattered over Al Anbar Province. It's unlikely that this is Daniel's group.

Then I remembered that, two days before, Daniel had sent us an e-mail mentioning he had just come back to the base after several days' patrol for some "down" time. Perhaps his platoon had not yet returned to patrol duty?

I checked his e-mail account. If e-mail sent in the past few hours had been opened, it meant he would have been safely on base at the time of the incident. Nervously I looked at his inbox and was disheartened to discover several days' worth of e-mails still unopened. My palms began to perspire and my adrenalin surged. I reminded myself that even if it *was* Daniel's battalion, that did not mean he had been involved in the incident.

Then, I opened an e-mail from Phyllis, a mom whose son was also in the same battalion:

> Prayers and hugs to all this sorrowful morning. As we wait
> for more news of our losses in the Fallujah car bombing, I
> know we are together in spirit and am so grateful once again
> for our group. God bless you all.

So she too assumed the bombing involved our sons. I could see that this day would be a very long one.

The bombing had occurred at approximately 11:00 PM Pacific Daylight Time—incredibly the same timeframe in which Mario had his dream. I wondered how long it could take for a casualty officer to get to our house to inform us if Daniel had been one of those killed. Allowing for a delay so that officials in Iraq could confirm the identities of the dead and organize a local bereavement team here in northern California, I speculated we might get word in twelve to sixteen hours after the incident—in other words, by the afternoon.

Mario and I now had a difficult time going to the memorial. We wanted to pay our respects, but it was all too easy to imagine that perhaps we might have to go through a similar ritual the next week.

Several parents from our Military Family Support Group also attended the memorial, had heard the news report, and offered their love and prayers. The mother of a man killed in action the previous year embraced and comforted me. It was as if everyone sensed Daniel's group was involved with this tragedy.

After a seemingly endless drive home, we took a deep cleansing breath and scanned the parked cars before we turned down our street. No Marine Corps vehicle.

At a turtle's pace the blistering afternoon crawled by. I tried to do things that ordinarily soothed me, reading or stitching, but I was too jittery. As my mind continuously wandered to the day's news, my panic would begin anew. Was there a mother somewhere just now learning her son was gone? By hoping for Daniel's safety, it felt as if I were hoping it was someone else's son who was dead. I knew I didn't want that; yet, I felt guilty all the same.

Many of our friends had been e-mailing, asking if we had heard anything. I hadn't looked at e-mail for the past twenty minutes—maybe there were some new ones? Maybe there was even an e-mail from Daniel? And I suppose now was as good a time as any to answer all the e-mails I'd been putting off.

And so it went. As afternoon dragged into evening, I began to feel more confident that the Angel of Death had bypassed our doorstep. Mario assured me, "If Daniel had been badly injured or killed in this, we would have gotten a visit by now. I think he's okay." By the time we went to bed, we dared to allow ourselves to feel relieved.

2 AM, September 7

The telephone shattered our sleep. It was Daniel. He was alive! "Thank you, God, thank you," I whispered.

"Choncho! Choncho!" I called to my husband, "It's Daniel! Pick up the other phone."

Daniel got right to the point. "It was our platoon which got hit."

"Oh no! We were afraid of that," I said. "Can you tell us what happened?"

His voice was sober and unemotional. "We were supposed to go relieve the 1st Platoon this morning. You know the open-top vehicles with the benches that face outward? Well, I always try to ride in the first vehicle when I go on convoys, and I sit just behind the driver. This time I climbed into the first truck to sit in my usual spot. As I sat in the vehicle, they stopped me and told me that we were splitting into squads, and they needed me to go in the second vehicle because I would be going to a different tower."

The tone of his voice abruptly became derisive. "The politicians don't want to piss the Iraqis off, so we've been told that we can't stop civilian traffic to allow our patrols to safely pass by.

"Everyone was going to work and we were caught in the slow Monday morning traffic. As our three vehicles crept along, I started to daydream. I was kind of aware of a car going faster and passing us.

"All of a sudden, I felt a concussion and then heard a huge explosion. Right away we raced out of our truck to investigate. A huge cloud of smoke covered all of the traffic lanes. As we got on the scene, hoping to find people still alive, I saw a fire in front of us.

"At first I thought that the other vehicle was okay, but as we raced to it, we could hear screaming and moaning. The stench of burning flesh was horrible! I knew that whatever we were headed for was going to be bad."

The phone began to tremble in my hand as I finally let out my breath.

"It was like a horror movie. Body parts all over the place. Legs, arms, little pieces of tissue and skin with bits of intestines and other stuff lying in the sand. Fragments of metal with tissue hanging from them.

"As I came up, I saw one Marine lying on the ground near the fireball. His head was several feet away. His eyes were open and staring. I looked around and saw bodies everywhere."

Daniel's voice was wooden, as if he was repeating a news story he'd heard.

"When I bent over one body to see who it was, I realized the head had separated and the neck was floppy like Jell-O."

"Honey, I'm so sorry," I whispered.

He continued, "There were two other bodies nearby, also decapitated. Further up, I saw a body on its back, with his face blown off. I went to see who else had been hit, and a friend had already reached the other body. The head was smashed in. I looked up at the smoldering truck. Others in our squad were reaching under the truck to grab the remains of a body. Burning oil had spilled onto the body, and it was shriveled and charred.

"Shortly after we got an accountability report for everyone, I looked across the street and saw another Marine lifting what looked like a deflated football. I called out, 'What is that?' He hollered back, 'You don't want to know.'

"Then I saw there was hair on it. That's when I realized it was the missing face and scalp of one of our friends.

Daniel's voice became fierce, "We lost an entire squad! We were only a month from coming home!"

Oh Daniel, I thought, you have just looked into the face of hell and you will never be the same.

Chapter One

MARIO'S STORY

Daniel's decision to be a Marine was not random. The Marine Corps had been a low-voltage current pulsing through our family life before he was born.

Mario Roberto Sagastume was born in 1947 in the capital city of Guatemala, the second of three sons born to Aminda and Victor Sagastume. When Mario's parents divorced, his father moved to Los Angeles. His mother stayed in Guatemala with eight year-old Mario and his younger brother Edgar (Mario's older brother, Luis, was already living with family friends in San Francisco). Mario's mother moved the little family to the small town of Sololá, where she worked as a public health nurse and midwife. She struggled to eke out a livelihood. Years later, when Mario and I drove by that house where he grew up, I was stunned to see how poor his circumstances had been.

Mario came to the United States at age fifteen to live with his father; the two of them lived more like roommates than parent and child. Victor was fluent in English but Mario knew none when he arrived. There were few English-as-a Second-Language classes in the early sixties. He learned the language within two months and credits his rapid facility to his exposure to English in the classroom and—he swears this is true—to watching television shows such as *Leave it to Beaver* and *Red Skelton*.

Within a few years Mario adapted to California life. While a student at Belmont High School in Los Angeles, he participated in school musicals and made new friends. In summer he surfed at nearby Pacific beaches in fashion: bleaching his dark brown hair blond and sporting a large surfer cross. He took his after-school job as a bus boy seriously, even bypassing his prom because he was needed at work. By the time he had graduated from high school, he had earned enough money to buy a little Datsun car. After graduation he registered for general education classes in junior college, but was an indolent student.

Because the Vietnam War was escalating—and since Mario's grades in junior college were lackluster—he knew he would not be eligible for a student deferment from the draft. Despite the fact that Mario was not a United States citizen, as a resident alien he was still required to register with the Selective Service System.

He had intended to enlist in the Navy when he dropped by the complex where the recruiting offices for all the military branches were located. The office for the Marine Corps caught his eye first and the Marine recruiter encouraged him to enlist. "After you become a Marine, all you have to do is put in your request to become a Security Guard at the American Embassy in Guatemala. I'm sure you'll get it." At nineteen, Mario was just naïve enough to believe such a statement. The prospect of being stationed in Guatemala, where he would be able to see extended family again, was tempting enough to convince Mario that the Marine Corps was for him. Oh, he got guard duty, all right—in the rice paddies of Vietnam.

Before long, he left his new Datsun with his dad for safekeeping and was on his way to boot camp at the Marine Corps Recruit Depot (MCRD) in San Diego. The moment he and the other recruits arrived by bus late at night, the drill instructor roared, "***Get off my bus!***" This is a time-honored command to every arriving busload. The recruits were then ordered to place their feet on yellow footprints painted on the sidewalk in front of the receiving area. It was at that moment that Mario began to entertain the notion he just may have made a big mistake.

During the mid-sixties, the usual twelve to thirteen weeks of boot camp training was compressed into nine in order to accommodate the needs of the Vietnam War. The training was—and is still today—rigorous, always preparing a recruit for the time when a Marine might find himself either in a war or perhaps a prisoner of war. Years later my husband remarked to me, "I don't regret any aspect of Marine Corps training. Even the stuff that seems too tough serves a purpose."

"But some of it seems cruel," I once objected. "What if someone can't handle the yelling or belittling? That could destroy a person."

"Do you think an enemy would be gentle?" he scoffed. "Trust me. The enemy would do far worse than anything a drill instructor might ever dish out in boot camp. Maybe the training seems cruel to civilians, but if a Marine becomes a prisoner of war, no enemy is going to be worrying about his fragile psyche!"

When he lived in Guatemala, Mario was accustomed to having few luxuries and to the necessity of hard work, so he did not find the rigors of boot camp as onerous as others did. One of the ways he coped with the demanding aspects of training was to see its absurdities. Farcical situations could range from recruits being ordered to rake grassy areas literally by hand—one leaf at a time—to the way in which drill instructors strung together colorful litanies of epithets and curse words. Of course it would have been ruinous for Mario to laugh out loud, but his sense of humor helped him cope.

In June of 1966, he graduated from boot camp, proudly earning the title of "United States Marine."

The training schedule after boot camp is different now, but, in Mario's time, new Marines went to Camp Pendleton right after graduation for Infantry Training Regiment, or ITR. The name is now "School of Infantry," or SOI. After completing four weeks of tactical field training at ITR and an additional two weeks' training at machine gun school, he was given a standard thirty-day pre-deployment leave. Then his Marine unit landed in Da Nang, Vietnam.

As far as he's aware, none of Mario's letters from Vietnam still exist. He thinks he wrote only a handful to family members, and he did not have a girlfriend to whom he needed to write regularly. He definitely wasn't a journal-keeper, and his reputation as a notoriously poor letter-writer still stands. His memories are the only souvenirs of his war experience.

For a few months Mario was a member of a security platoon at the Marine base in Da Nang, but eventually he was assigned as a combat replacement to the 2nd Battalion, 1st Regiment of the 1st Marine Division, serving with Fox Company's 3rd Platoon. Although the entire battalion comprised approximately one thousand men, the group of forty men in Fox Company's 3rd Platoon—and specifically his squad, an even smaller group—became his family.

As a platoon machine gunner, Mario's responsibility was to augment firepower. Gunners were favorite targets of the enemy; for the first time in his life, Mario's short stature became an advantage. The Viet Cong, expecting Americans to be taller, aimed their weapons higher; Mario's smaller frame provided a less prominent target.

"Vietnam is a really pretty country. It reminded me a bit of Guatemala. Even the poor people were like poor people in Guatemala. I think the transition was easier for me than for other Marines."

Despite the lush beauty of the countryside, Mario found the hot and humid weather difficult to cope with. He sweated profusely. Once, while on patrol, he needed to be medivacced for heat exhaustion. Intravenous fluids quickly restored him and he returned to the field. Fortunately, that was the extent of his war injuries.

He tends to be dismissive about his combat exposure, saying that he didn't see the amount of combat that troops who served later in the war did. In the late sixties, the U.S. death toll would frequently reach five hundred men per *week*. In one month during the Vietnam War, we experienced the same number of American casualties as we suffered in the first *year* of Operation Iraqi Freedom.

As an infantryman, Mario participated in major operations and he patrolled the Vietnamese countryside, always carefully scanning the road for mines or booby traps. He also took his turn standing watch for the platoon. As a machine gunner, he was called upon to return enemy fire. He killed enemy fighters, but his platoon also took prisoners. Helicopters were a means of transportation of troops and supplies as well as evacuation of the wounded. Mario still finds the whump-whump sound of helicopter blades chopping through the air disturbing. The sound reminds him of the vulnerability he faced each time he and the others had to step out in the open landing zone, fully exposed to the enemy, in order to off-load supplies from helicopters and on-load casualties. All these years later, he is disconcerted by a sense of déjà-vu whenever he passes the many rice fields near our home.

His tour was punctuated by fatigue, boredom, fear, and brotherhood. "We didn't have e-mail or satellite phones. Unless there was a dire emergency, there were no phone calls to family. We just had each other. If someone's girlfriend dumped him, he talked about it with his buddy. He couldn't call home.

"I think it's better that way. Because today's combat Marines can keep in frequent contact by phones and web-cams, it keeps them attached to their families and inhibits being there for each other. They're more likely to stay homesick. I think all that family contact sets them up to become over-involved with their families' day-to-day problems. That's not good for them."

One story Mario tells illustrates the depth of the brotherhood and chills me to this day. On a moonless night, when his platoon headed out for patrol, they stopped at a river they needed to ford. The Marines could hear the Viet Cong on the opposite bank, so it was imperative they move silently. Mario's group slipped, single file, into the river. The river bottom was uneven, and when he was partway across, Mario realized the water would soon cover his nose.

"Even though my friend Kelly was somewhere behind me, I knew I didn't dare call out. That might have alerted the enemy to our presence, and I couldn't take that chance. Treading water wasn't an option either; that would have been too noisy."

Mario shrugged matter-of-factly. "So I figured I'd rather quietly drown instead. That was better than endangering the guys with me.

"But, just as the water reached my nose and I was about to go under, I felt a hand grab the back of my flak jacket, and I felt myself being pulled up and propelled to the other side of the river."

For thirty-eight years Mario tried to locate the platoon buddy who saved him, and he finally did so. We met this man and he has corroborated this story. Though he couldn't see Mario in the intense darkness, he knew that he was somewhere in front.

"I'm a lot taller than Mario. I knew that if the water was becoming too deep for me, Mario had to be in trouble."

I offer this anecdote as a tribute to the extraordinary loyalty and sense of brotherhood with which Marines are imbued: that allowing oneself to drown would be preferable to imperiling Marine brothers.

When a Marine's thirteen-month "in country" tour was completed, he was taken out of the fields of Vietnam and flown home. Every individual was on a different schedule. In October 1967, Mario was plucked from his platoon, leaving behind buddies who had not completed their tours. One day he was in a war; the next day, he was flown to the United States.

No one was waiting at Travis Air Force Base to greet him. "I don't remember whether I even told my family when I was coming home."

He took a commercial bus the fifty miles to San Francisco where he spent a few days with his older brother before going to see his dad in Los Angeles.

Mario still had two more years to complete in the Marine Corps, which he did as a supply clerk at Camp Pendleton. In January of 1969, his request for an "early out" from the Marine Corps was granted, allowing him to enroll for the spring semester at the University of San Francisco. Since the GI bill helped with only some of the tuition fee, Mario took a job washing dishes in the University's dining hall to supplement his income.

The morning of September 15, 1969, when I arrived for breakfast at the close of the dining hall's mealtime, few students remained. As I sat down next to an acquaintance, I noticed someone wearing a large white apron, one of the kitchen staff. He leaned back in his chair, absentmindedly tapping a smoldering lump of ash from his cigarette against the silver foil ashtray. He was stocky but muscular, and his manner gave him an air of being larger than his five-foot, three-inch frame. His eyes were dark brown and seductive. A well-trimmed mustache bristled across his upper lip. As I was introduced to Mario, I noticed he was polite—even courtly. Since my primary-grade days, when I drooled over the popular romantic television character Zorro, I had harbored a secret fantasy of a Latin dream man. Here he was! From our first meeting I was smitten.

Chapter Two

My Story

I was born in Alexandria, Virginia, in 1950, the younger of two daughters of John and Virginia Magrath. Alexandria is a town rich in Revolutionary and Civil War history. Unlike anyone in my family, I was a history devotee. Geographic intimacy with those places and the artifacts associated with significant events in our nation's past thrilled me. I got goose bumps to realize that I walked where George Washington or Robert E. Lee had actually walked, or I stood where Lincoln had watched a play at Ford's Theater. The nearby battlefields of Manassas and Gettysburg captivated me. My sense of the historical also extended to a resolute patriotism. In grade school, I kept parchment paper copies of the Declaration of Independence and the Constitution on my bedroom wall and made a point of reading them every Fourth of July.

I attended a private all-girls' high school—sadly, no longer in existence —the Academy of Notre Dame in Washington, D.C. In traveling to my school, located near the Capitol building, I passed many historical landmarks each day. Depending on which bus route I chose, I might pass the Lincoln Memorial, the Jefferson Memorial—exquisite when the cherry blossoms were in bloom—or the Pentagon. I cherished those architectural symbols of our country. To this day, whenever I gaze at the monuments and symbols of our country, I am filled with a surge of love for our nation.

In the summer after my graduation from high school, I traveled with other students from my high school and my French teacher as part of a larger tour to French-speaking countries in Europe. We spent three weeks in Leysin, Switzerland, and three weeks in Brussels, Belgium, with side trips to other European countries. In several of the countries (notably in Cologne, Germany) evidence of damage during World War II was still apparent, even more than twenty years later, underscoring for me the destruction of war, which I took to heart.

This travel opportunity allowed me, in a limited way, to experience living in another country, communicating in a foreign tongue, and handling the feelings of being homesick. Traveling and living abroad, even for that brief time, helped me to be more sensitive to immigrants—an advantage to me when I eventually met my future husband.

After my high school graduation, my family moved to the West Coast. I was in my second year in the nursing program at the University of San Francisco when I met Mario.

The frayed green field jacket with his name on its pocket revealed he had been in the Marines Corps, and I learned he'd been in Vietnam. The Vietnam War was the topic of much divisive national dispute, and I was curious to hear his thoughts. His response to various inquiries, however, was typically a verbal parry, telling one superficial story to one person and a contradictory one to another. He made it sound as if he had never seen action. But, in fact, he just didn't want to talk about it. He especially didn't want to engage in a political debate. When he met my mother, he minimized his role altogether; he didn't want to be caught in a discussion with my mother, who had a habit of skewering people with her questions. This reluctance to speak of his war experience and avoidance of discussions, I later learned, can be a symptom of Post-Traumatic Stress Disorder (PTSD).

Though he intrigued me, I was also a little apprehensive about this twenty-two year old man who had worldly knowledge of other countries, of war, and, I presumed, of women. After all, I was a sheltered, naïve, and innocent nineteen-year-old Catholic girl. His life experience lent him a wisdom and maturity that others his age didn't have. Despite my nervousness about him, his personality and the chemistry of our diametrical natures sufficiently attracted me that I continued to go out with him for the next three years. While I finished nursing school, he worked full-time by day and was an indifferent student at the University's evening college.

Mario frequently scanned his environment, keeping track of anyone in his vicinity. Many times he scolded that my walking down city streets, inattentive to my surroundings, was unwise and unsafe. I noticed his need to sit with his back to the wall while in public places, in order to see who came in or out. Mario admits he occasionally still conducts a mini-safety patrol of a new environment, or, as he wryly calls it, "checks the perimeter."

On freeways Mario tended to drive his sporty Datsun convertible faster than the speed limit permitted. When I protested, he would retort, "Don't you trust me? Do you think I would let us crash?" Instead of my concern being an issue of safety, he turned it into a test of trust. If another driver cut him off in traffic, he would become furious, curse loudly, and frequently would speed up to tailgate the offender. Sometimes Mario pulled alongside the other driver and turned a menacing glare on him. I was frightened.

Irritability, anger, hyper-arousal or hyper-vigilance, pugnacity, alcohol and other substance abuse, hypersensitivity to injustice—I later learned are symptoms consistent with PTSD. Knowing what I know now, I would interpret Mario's behaviors as signs of the disorder.

Many of his friends drank heavily and smoked marijuana at parties. In San Francisco in the late sixties and early seventies, that was not so unusual but, by his own admission, Mario drank excessively during his last two years in the service. Not being a drinker or a user, I didn't have a concept of how much of these substances constituted "too much."

Mario took offense if someone looked at him the "wrong" way, or seemed to act in a manner that suggested racial prejudice toward him—even when I didn't agree with his interpretation of the situation. He seemed to have a chip on his shoulder.

One time, while riding a cable car, another passenger looked at Mario with what he deemed to be a disapproving glance. He jerked his head at the stranger and growled, "Do you have a problem?" I honestly don't remember that the man had said or done anything provocative. Mario, however, challenged him to a fight. I was appalled and embarrassed. I kept saying, "Let it go. Let's just get off the trolley." We had arrived at our destination and debarked, but now Mario was angry with me for trying to interfere in the situation. He felt he'd lost face, "How do you think I feel? It looks like I let my woman run things in front of this guy." His belligerence confused and frightened me. There were similar incidents in which he took umbrage at people's facial expressions or manner. In my ignorance, I attributed the incidents to his "hot-blooded Latin" temperament. Lacking brothers, I assumed I was merely unfamiliar with what must be common—though to me, mysterious—behaviors of the male species. It never occurred to me to wonder until after we were married if there was a connection to his wartime experience.

Despite these blips on the radar screen, the overall essence of Mario was—and is—warm, magnetic, affectionate, funny, generous, and thoughtful. There was substance and depth to him. The exposure to his family and to his culture broadened my perspective and enriched me. We married in September of 1972.

Chapter Three

OUR STORY

Even though Mario and I had known each other for three years prior to our marriage, making a home with him was an adventure. I worked full time as a staff nurse in the Bay Area for the first few years. Mario, having dropped out of college the year before our wedding, worked at a series of full-time jobs. By the time we were married, my parents lived only thirty miles away, and Mario's immediate family—his two brothers and their significant others, his sister and her family, his mother, and his father—all lived in the same city as we did. Mario and I attended the gatherings his mother held weekly for her family as well as her frequent cross-generational parties, which featured lots of Latin music and dancing.

Nonetheless, before our first anniversary, we started to experience relationship difficulties. Unlike the early days of courting, during the early years of marriage Mario was increasingly moody and emotionally—though never physically—abusive to me.

In many ways the discord in our marriage mirrored the disharmony in our country during the early seventies. Mario began to rebel against American culture as being typically avaricious, superficial, and lacking true family values.

There were large-scale protests against the Vietnam War, which sometimes resulted in violence. Cynicism regarding the credibility of government and the integrity of police was swelling against the backdrop of the Watergate debacle, racial riots, and claims of "police brutality." Younger and older generations saw each other as alien and incomprehensible. Against this adversarial and often hostile backdrop, Mario, like many people at the time, distrusted any agent of traditional authority. After years of regimentation in the Marine Corps, he was particularly scathing of the government and derided any gesture of patriotism.

As a young married couple, our social set consisted mostly of Mario's family members and friends. Mario did not much like being with my American friends; he thought they were snooty. Our two families didn't socialize either; the language barrier was a significant obstacle to bridging the conspicuous social disparities between the families.

Not being a marijuana user or a drinker, I was something of a social misfit in Mario's world. He scoffed at how "uptight" I was and scolded me for judging marijuana without even trying it.

I tried to disguise my personal discomfort with pot smoking by framing it as fear of losing my nursing license if I was ever caught. I didn't know for sure if that was true, but it sounded plausible enough. I hoped I could dodge Mario's scorn using this rationale, but it didn't work.

Over time, Mario's marijuana use increased, alarming me. When we first married, because I had an aversion to the scent, I tried to make a rule that he could smoke marijuana only on the porch outside our apartment. He would have none of it.

"It's my home too! And if I want to smoke in the house, I will. I don't need your permission. You're not my mother!"

When I remonstrated that I was worried that he smoked too much marijuana, he sneered, "Oh come *on*, Nanette, you're worried about that little bit? If I start to smoke several joints a week, then you can worry. Get off my back!"

When he reached the several-joints-a-week milestone, I confronted him. He protested that he didn't have a substance-abuse problem, and set a new criterion for alarm. "Don't worry unless you see me smoking every day. Then you can worry."

Over the next year, he breached and reset the bar until he was smoking several joints a day. As his marijuana use accelerated, he began to skip classes at the vocational business college he attended.

Substance abuse, leading to failure to fulfill obligations in school, is referenced as a symptom associated with PTSD in *Courage After Fire* (Armstrong, Best, and Domenici, 2006, 27).

Since Mario often argued that I shouldn't judge marijuana if I had never tried it, sometime in the second year of marriage I reluctantly agreed.

Even that became an occasion for argument; Mario was irritated when I couldn't figure out how to inhale.

"Come *on*, Nanette! All you have to do is breathe it all the way down into your lungs. Aw, don't hold it in your mouth, for Christ's sake! Come on, take another toke and see if you can do it right this time. Hurry up; you're going to waste the whole joint at this rate."

I couldn't stand the feeling of breathing a substance into my lungs, yet I wanted to do this and get it over with. In the end, I wasted the majority of the joint—much to Mario's exasperation—leaving only the roach end, which Mario inhaled so it wouldn't go to waste.

I did a mental self-check. Since I didn't feel different, I presumed that I hadn't inhaled any of the marijuana. A little later, while washing my hands in the bathroom sink, I absent-mindedly glanced in the mirror. Two dull and glassy eyes stared back. Apparently, I had managed to inhale enough after all. I had never even been drunk before; yet there I was stoned. I was very disappointed with myself; that person in the mirror was not me. I still regret that I threw my own values overboard rather than risk Mario's displeasure with me.

Increasingly, Mario ridiculed my family, telling me their interactions with each other were "weird" and that they were weird. He belittled us as "typically American," which sometimes meant "typically white." His own family's values, on the other hand, he considered exemplary. He taunted me from time to time for being a college graduate, sneering, "I guess I'm not a smart college graduate like you."

I wasn't able to undo my college degree. I certainly couldn't do anything about being a white American, nor could I change who my parents were. After hearing these comments often, I began to be ashamed of who I was. Over time, Mario's frequent scorn began to tear away at my self-image; I began to feel defective for my values, my family, my tastes, my desires. My response to this was to try even harder to please. I made an effort to be tolerant when he said rude things. But I hurt.

The only time that I have ever been tempted to stray from my marriage vows was during this period. A young medical resident at the hospital began to flirt flamboyantly with me; it was flattering to be desired rather than picked at. The allure was strong enough that I told Mario, "You might want to start treating me better. A doctor at the hospital likes me. He's starting to look pretty good to me, and I'm tempted."

Fortunately, I decided that any solace I might receive from an affair would not be worth the pain it would cause all of us. For his part, Mario was sufficiently alarmed by my comment that he curbed his scornful remarks.

Mario continued to balk at all rules—whether "house" rules or governmental ones—and, indeed, at any social conventions, such as dress codes. I recall being embarrassed that he would not change his sloppy overalls to go with me to an upscale performance at the San Francisco Opera House. There was tension and much pain in our relationship during those days. I knew most of our friends did not expect our marriage to survive. Before we were married, citing all the differences between us, my mother had even tried to talk me out of getting married. That only reinforced my resolve. I refused to fail at marriage.

I made an appointment for us with a marriage counselor. During the initial intake appointment, I remember the counselor laughing and saying, "Most of my clients have trouble agreeing whether they will live in Burlingame or Hillsborough [Bay Area cities]. But you guys can't even agree which country to live in!" Indeed, Mario wanted to get away from America, which he disdained, and move to Guatemala. On the other hand, I was reluctant to live outside the United States.

Our having such dissimilar views also extended to our perceptions about the state of our relationship. These discrepancies only aggravated our emotional turmoil. By the winter of 1973 I observed in my journal:

> [Today] Mario and I had a hard talk about our relationship.
> I am enjoying him more and feel better about us than before.
> [So] I was stunned when he told me that he feels more
> discouraged.... He started to say things calmly like, "I

don't think you and I are working out." This unhinges me, coming just as I am feeling more hopeful about us. When we have the same old problems, he thinks that means we aren't meant for each other. I look upon it more philosophically [that our problem areas will always be with us]. Still, when he says things like this, it makes me anxious and insecure.

After all these years, that level of divergence between our tastes and perceptions is still the same. What is different now is that we know to expect it and we are able to joke about it.

I remember asking the counselor whether he thought there was a link between Mario's anger and his combat exposure. The counselor dismissed any such connection. PTSD was not a recognized condition—much less a diagnosis—until years later. I recall the counselor implying that Mario was having a delayed/prolonged phase of teenage rebellion (at the age of twenty-six, no less). I was unable to articulate it, but I felt certain in my bones that Mario's animosity to the military and the government, as well as his pugnacity and rebellion against any conformity to social conventions, were in reaction to his military experience.

In fairness, the counselor could only function with the sparse amount of information that was available at the time regarding post-combat adjustment. He coached us in communication techniques, and that did help us maintain our relationship during these rocky years.

Mario himself didn't feel there was anything inappropriate about his behavior or that there was any correlation between his anger and his wartime service, but by this time I felt certain that somehow the anger was displaced emotion. During these years he was very irritable. Throughout our life together he has had a tendency toward tantrums, getting overly angry at events both large and small. He has never hit me; indeed, I warned him that if he did, I would leave him. He has, however, occasionally thrown objects at a safe target in my vicinity. And he raises his voice. I still get frightened at the timbre of his voice. I recently found an apt quote from *Down Range: To Iraq and Back* by Bridget Cantrell, Ph.D. and Chuck Dean, about post-combat adjustment for today's combat vets:

Anger can also be expressed non-verbally and be quite intimidating to those who are the targets of … rage. They [vets] have no idea how intimidating [they] can appear just by … body posture, and … eye contact. To appear frightening and out of control, words need not even be exchanged…. (Cantrell and Dean 2005, 41).

Mario himself feared the power of his anger. For the first decade of our marriage, he would often cut off my attempts to argue an issue with him by barking, "Don't make me angry! I might not be able to control myself. I don't want to hurt you!" Though his plea left me suffocating on my own need to speak, I believe his words were not a manipulative ploy, but reflected a genuine fear that his rage might overwhelm him. I took elaborate pains to avoid angering him or voicing a viewpoint contrary to his. It was oddly comforting to me when I recently came across a passage discussing the effects of trauma on the central nervous system in a book by Dr. Aphrodite Matsakis. in *Vietnam Wives*. She states:

When family members of veterans with PTSD 'walk on eggs', it is because they do not want to trigger their veteran into a rage reaction over which he may not have control…. The Vietnam wife … like her children, may attribute the veteran's mood swings and rage reactions to her behavior. Yet one of the prime causes of these symptoms lies in the changes in the veteran's biochemistry due to overuse of his emergency biological system (Matsakis, 1996, 52,53).

There was a point, in the second or third year of marriage, that I made a deliberate decision to allow Mario to say those ugly things to me without censuring him. If getting his anger out would provide catharsis, then I was convinced that I loved him enough and was strong enough to be able to take the abuse. I would be the lightning rod through which his high-voltage anger could be defused. I hoped this would relieve some of his pain.

This decision was fortuitous for him; it did help him. It was, however, a bad decision for me. Yes, I did "take it," but his anger scarred my heart. I was fearful of his temper tantrums, anxious that if I didn't please, he would yell or, worse, leave me. In order to avoid his emotional abuse, I spent a lot of time hiding many of my real thoughts and opinions—a pattern I continued for decades. For a very long time, I lost who I was. There is, even now, a part of me that sometimes still withholds myself from him in an automatic, self-protective gesture. Obviously, I still have work to do in this area.

I now realize I should have just said to him, "Honey, I love you, but you may not treat me like this." If I had defined my boundaries for impermissible behavior, I could have placed limits on it. As it was, I did not define what was unacceptable behavior towards me and thus I ensured it. Mario and I were pretty much on our own dealing with this. Because PTSD was not a recognized diagnosis then, there were no treatment suggestions, no guidelines for family members, and, at that time, no veterans' support groups.

When Mario looks back to those days of our early marriage, he sorrowfully acknowledges that he was hurtful. Moreover, he credits me for "saving his life" in those years. He truly believes that were it not for me, "I would be dead on the street" from alcohol or drug abuse. But if I were to be placed back in time, I would do it differently—in a way that would have maintained my integrity and self-respect.

How much of Mario's emotional reactions were due to his cultural background or his substance abuse, I am not sure. But I do feel that, in no small measure, his behavior arose from thirteen months of fearing for his life and seeing death up close. Constant danger, being shot at, inability to distinguish the enemy, seeing friends injured or killed are situations which certainly result in psychological trauma.

After what I have said about Mario, it might seem incomprehensible that I saw enough good qualities to justify staying married to him. But I think that we are the quintessential yin and yang. I balance Mario's impulsivity. He is able to make a decision quickly—but often changes it. I struggle to make the "right" decision as if, once made, it could never be changed. Yet, having painstakingly considered all aspects of a decision, I seldom need to change my mind. He tends to be the dreamer; I am the realist. He's the adventurer; I am timorous. He is flexible; I tend to be rule-bound. He vents his emotions freely; I tend to control mine. While not blind to the need for money, he also considers that it is there to be enjoyed; he has been lavishly generous with it.

I am stingier. I provide stable predictability and organization to his life. He prevents me from being stagnant and dour by adding fun and spontaneity to my life.

One of Mario's best qualities is his sense of humor. He brings a refreshing levity to ticklish situations; he is able to laugh at himself.

I believe that we have been given to each other as partners to stimulate the other's growth, by challenging each other's comfort zone. Over the years, with the help of counselors, we have worked on our "stuff" and have become less dysfunctional than we were in the early years. In spite of the discord, I focused in the early years on the person I knew Mario was capable of being. I also realize now that was a high-stakes gamble. One should never count on another to change or reform. Fortunately for me, once he began to tame his demons, Mario's wonderful qualities blossomed.

Because there were so many disparities in our relationship, I have had to stretch myself to accommodate another point of view—one that is frequently very different from mine. There is no coasting allowed in our relationship, as might have been possible had we been of similar background, expectations, and opinions. We have had to work at our relationship all the time. Mario is bright, charming, funny, affectionate, and is an excellent family man. He is very generous and warm-hearted. He is courageously humble enough to allow me to publish these stories that are so uncomplimentary to him. In fact, he has encouraged me because he believes in the value of my story. He is my dearest friend.

Though I know that one could ascribe much of Mario's behavior to his inborn temperament, Latin machismo, or any number of conditions, there is a convergence of symptoms that also suggest Post Traumatic Stress Disorder. On the only occasion his mother Aminda spoke of this, she wept while confiding to me that her son had changed significantly since going to war. Unlike the happy-go-lucky youngster who joked and laughed often, he was now a very serious person.

Her words convinced me that it probably was better that I never knew Mario before he went to Vietnam. Not knowing him before the war meant that I had no expectations that he would return the same person. I was in a position to accept him the way he was, his "new normal."

Post-Traumatic Stress Disorder, or PTSD, was first listed as a diagnosis in the Third Edition of the Diagnostic and Statistical Manual (DSM) of the American Psychiatric Association in 1980. The diagnostic criteria for this diagnosis have been refined since that time. In the book *Down Range: From Iraq and Back*, PTSD is not described as a mental illness, but as a reaction to an unusual traumatic event in which a person experienced, witnessed, or was confronted with death or serious injury, or a threat of the same to others. Some combat veterans might suffer PTSD, but so might victims of disaster, violence, or abuse.

Only recently has Mario disclosed that he has had a constant sense of sadness ever since his return from Vietnam. He admits that he could cry at any given moment if he allowed himself to think about his experiences. He believes that the sadness is rooted in more than one aspect of his combat experience but predominantly is caused by survivor guilt. Wondering why his life has been spared, when others who deserved, perhaps even more, to live, but were not as fortunate, is a painful enigma many veterans face.

Perhaps many of Mario's PTSD behaviors were efforts to push away the guilt. Perhaps he subconsciously reacted to ever-present sadness with an overlay of anger. Even Mario isn't sure.

Over the years, he has come to realize that the sadness probably will never leave him, and he needs to put it aside so that he can go on with his life. He has chosen to allow the sadness out and to weep only at specific, emotionally safe times—such as at his veterans' reunions.

When our son Daniel became a Marine, and particularly when he deployed to Iraq, Mario's sadness was intensified by fear for his son. For Mario, having his son in danger was more painful than when he himself had been the one going into combat.

In rereading my journal entries from the early years, the atmosphere of tension and anxiety pervading our household during the first decade or so of our marriage assailed me. Any household calm was only a precarious veneer, though the tension level was not as apparent to me at the time.

I have some discomfort in having given such an intimate portrait of our lives, but to merely mention that Mario had PTSD seems inadequate. People can easily recognize that a veteran who barricades himself with weapons inside his house needs help. But what does the disorder look like when it is less conspicuous and the sufferer is functioning productively in life? My motive in disclosing this kind of detail about our relationship is to illustrate that, even when mild, PTSD is not harmless. Untended PTSD affects more than just the warrior.

PTSD permeated our household, and affected not only my husband and me, but all our children. PTSD that is not confronted leaves a toxic soup that poisons the entire family. My experience has led to my belief that the earlier a veteran addresses post-combat stress, the less severe the effect might be on his family and on future generations of that family.

I am glad that Mario has taken steps to heal. I can only wish that he had done it sooner in our life together. I am not able to discern yet all the ways that PTSD affected our family. I do know that, in an effort to emulate his father, Daniel has also imitated his moods and behaviors.

When my daughter was in her teens, she became involved in an unhealthy relationship in which there was emotional abuse. Though I tried to help her see that her relationship was unhealthy, I was perturbed that perhaps I had modeled acquiescence in the face of emotional abuse when she was little. If there had been earlier intervention into the PTSD, would we have been able to avoid the negative behaviors being passed to another generation?

Sometimes we sought counseling as a family, sometimes as a couple, sometimes individually. One psychologist, Judy Brislain, has guided our family intermittently for more than twenty-five years. The efforts of counselors have helped us keep our marriage and family intact. When Mario finally acknowledged he had post-combat issues and began to deal with them, things gradually got healthier at home.

One experience that helped our relationship in the first childless years of marriage was a three-month car trip to Guatemala in 1974. For Mario, it was going home—a home he hadn't seen for eleven years. For me, it was the chance to experience the family and culture that had shaped him. We were part of a multi-vehicle caravan of family members and friends, traveling twelve hours a day for a week. The long drives afforded Mario and me the opportunity to spend time together in an environment devoid of the usual encumbrances of chores, jobs, or routines. We had time to talk through issues but, more importantly, the trip offered us new and fun-filled experiences to share. The relaxed schedule allowed us time in which to appreciate being together.

When we began our trip, I wasn't sure our marriage would survive so much togetherness. But by the time of our return, we were on stronger footing. Not too long after our trip, Mario's drug use began to diminish; he cut his shoulder-length hair, put away his baggy denim overalls, bought two business suits, and found a bookkeeping job. I took a job with morning shift hours, Monday through Friday, at a blood plasma center.

We began to talk about having children. He was anxious to start a family. I was less sure about having a child yet; I wasn't convinced that our marriage was solid, or that I was ready to give up my personal freedom. Mario argued, "There are never any guarantees in life. If you waited till everything was perfect, you'd never do anything. You've got to take a chance sometimes."

I didn't want to have children and then watch our marriage dissolve a short time later. Mario countered, "One of the most painful things in my life was my parents' divorce. I was eight years old. That was just the worst pain ever. I don't want to ever do that to my children. I promise that I will do everything to keep that from happening."

So, with some anxious, yet delicious, anticipation, I got pregnant two months later. Mario made many changes in his behavior. Not only had he been a pot smoker, he had been a one- to two-pack-a-day tobacco smoker for nearly fifteen years. He had previously made several attempts to quit smoking. This time he stopped cold turkey and hasn't smoked a cigarette since. He occasionally smoked marijuana after I got pregnant, but it was an infrequent habit. I haven't seen him smoke pot for many years.

Mario also decided to return to college to obtain a bachelor's degree in accounting. He worked part time and went to school during my pregnancy.

Our first son, Mario Alejandro, was born in February of 1976. Four months after his birth we moved to Chico, California. There we could live more frugally while my husband attended the local university on the GI bill. In 1978, he graduated with a degree in accounting from California State University, Chico. I had been working two days a week at a local hospital, but several years later took a position at the University's Student Health Center. In 1980 I pursued additional education to obtain a nurse practitioner certificate in college health and worked in this capacity four days a week until I retired in 2006.

Mario and I had a second son, Damián Antonio, born in June of 1979. Our son Daniel Andrés was born in February of 1983. Throughout these busy years Mario was building a successful career in the grocery business and was doing very well under the wing of a prominent grocery-business entrepreneur. Much later Mario went on to own, in partnership, several grocery stores in the same franchise and more recently, an indoor soccer arena.

By the time our daughter, Clarissa Raquel, was born in 1984, Mario was working approximately sixty hours a week—occasionally more—in the grocery business. After a forty-minute commute, his eleven-hour workday began at 5:30 AM. The long day left him tired and cranky when he came home. Since his day started so early, he was in bed by 9:00 PM, but he was easily awakened by light or noise (difficulty sleeping and hypersensitivity to noise is a symptom of PTSD). The rest of the family was still awake at that hour. We were a busy household; Mario's sleep was not uncommonly interrupted by our communal noise. All of us can remember a number of occasions in which Mario awakened from sleep and stomped down the hall, threatening a spanking to those children who were not in bed yet or who were making noise.

Four active children with two parents working long hours meant the family stress and noise levels were high. Mario had very little patience; he snapped at the kids a lot. Indeed, trying to manage a household, work, and four children—several of whom had chronic medical problems—frazzled me. I know I got pretty irritable myself and did my own share of yelling. I think I managed to better control my temper in the last decade or so when the children were teenagers. By that time, *they* were the ones who were doing the yelling.

Despite these flaws, Mario was a good dad. He was very affectionate with his children, helped coach their soccer teams, went to their school programs, and was clearly interested in them. My earlier vision of his potential was prescient after all.

By this time—the early eighties—there was more information about PTSD symptoms; I felt certain that Mario's irritability, anger outbursts, and trouble sleeping suggested the disorder. When I asked Mario to consider going to some veterans' groups, he declined. I got the names of some counselors for him, but he denied the need for any outside assistance. "I can take care of this myself; I don't need anyone telling me how to think," he would respond. Perhaps he could handle it, but *we* were having trouble with his way of handling it.

A co-worker lent me a book that her Vietnam vet brother had felt was a realistic depiction of his time there. The book was *Nam*, by Mark Baker. I tried to interest Mario in the book, but he disdained it. I read it with much interest. It was the first time I'd been introduced to any first-hand accounts of the war in Vietnam.

By seeing combat through the eyes of someone who had known it, I hoped to understand Mario's experience. The book, and others that followed, allowed me a glimpse of what life was like for these men. Before long, Mario's curiosity was piqued and he too read *Nam*.

As more books about the war were marketed, Mario began to gulp them down. We started to build a home library of Vietnam War books. Movies followed several years later. In particular, a scene near the beginning of *Platoon* affected me. The protagonist lies in the dense foliage of the jungle; his fear of the enemy was so palpable that I became anxious myself. Invariably, by the conclusion of each new movie about Vietnam, Mario sobbed; yet, each time he cried there was more healing.

During these years, the "Moving Wall" (a portable and smaller traveling replica of the Vietnam Veteran's Memorial wall) toured in Chico. The experience of viewing that wall was also very emotional for him.

I knew Mario's healing was significant when he became a naturalized citizen on February 12, 1986. I appreciate how momentous a step it was to give up citizenship of his beloved homeland; I don't think I could ever give up my American citizenship. What a change from the first years of our marriage.

Long before we ever moved to Chico, there had been a traditional annual parade that featured local groups and marching bands from the surrounding area. The annual parade became defunct in the early eighties, but was revived in 1987. I decided that, since Vietnam vets had never had a homecoming parade, perhaps this new parade could correct that oversight. I filed an entry registration, and then tried to recruit veterans to march. Mario warned me, "Hon, I know you've worked hard and you mean well, but I don't think many vets will show up. Many are suspicious of the public after the way America received them. I really appreciate what you're doing, but I don't want you to be disappointed." Indeed, if other veterans or the city itself had sponsored this event, it might have increased its appeal. A co-worker and I worked to get it publicized.

I found a brown service shirt in the military surplus store, sewed Mario's "Corporal" chevrons on the sleeves, and put his name on it.

His family came to town to support him on the day of the parade, which, as luck would have it, was rainy. I had no idea whether my grand idea would be a dud. In the end, in addition to Mario and my co-worker's husband, eight or nine male vets and one female vet showed up. It was a rather ragtag group of people—most wearing only part of their original uniform—but I was pleased that at least some vets turned out. I was particularly thrilled to hear onlookers applaud as the vets marched past.

The following year vets marched again in the parade. Our three boys proudly joined Mario, and Daniel wore one of Mario's utility blouses.

From the late eighties onward, an increasing number of healing opportunities for veterans appeared. In 1988 California unveiled its own California Vietnam Veterans Memorial in Sacramento. All Vietnam veterans were invited to attend the ceremonies and to participate in a parade. Mario and I traveled to Sacramento for the weekend, staying at a sponsoring hotel. When we checked in, we realized there was scarcely a non-veteran guest at the hotel. The atmosphere was as gleeful as a giant slumber party.

Everywhere we went, at the hotel or even around town, there were Vietnam veterans, crying out greetings such as, "Welcome Home, Brother!" Over the years since the war, there had been some grousing and resentment about the "rear-echelon pogues;" that is the derisive epithet for those servicemen who never saw combat, had air-conditioned offices, daily showers, and ate real meals instead of C- rations. At this celebration, though, I didn't see any negativity. It didn't matter if a vet was a "grunt" or a "pogue"; the greeting was a heart-felt "Welcome home!" On the day of the dedication, my husband marched down the street with thousands of other vets who were cheered by the onlookers.

Several months later, in 1989, because my high school was scheduled to close forever—after being in existence for a hundred and sixteen years—an ultimate, all-classes reunion was scheduled. I hadn't been in Washington, DC for twenty years. Mario and I decided to turn my school reunion into a vacation. We left the younger two children with relatives and took Mario and Damián, ages thirteen and ten, with us. Since neither the children nor Mario had ever been to Washington, DC, we squeezed as much sightseeing as we could possibly do in seven days. Our first priority, within hours of arriving in Washington, was to visit the Vietnam Memorial. I prepared the boys, explaining to them how important it was to be reverent and to whisper when visiting the site. I also warned them that their dad might cry, and, if he did, that it was healthy and that he would be okay.

The evening of our arrival we walked to the area of the Ellipse near the Lincoln Memorial. Mario and I solemnly viewed a panel etched with the names of the eleven Fox Company Marines killed during Operation Union and for whom Mario was one of the combat replacements. Mario began to sob. Our children held his hand and hugged him. They were sweetly solicitous. We were at "The Wall" for quite a long time that evening. The boys made rubbings of the names of Marines that Mario knew. I made a rubbing of the name of Cathy Lane, the first nurse to be killed as a result of enemy fire. We went to the memorial several times during that trip and each time Mario seemed to release a little more sadness for his own experiences as well as for those persons whose names are on the wall. He said these emotions were mingled with a feeling of relief—which was quickly followed by guilt—that his own name is not on the Wall.

A significant event in Mario's healing was when Mario located a fledgling group of Vietnam veterans specifically from his Marine unit (2nd Battalion, 1st Marines). In 1991 Mario and I traveled to Washington, DC for a Veterans Day/ Marine Corps Birthday reunion of these Marines from his unit. As soon as Mario completed his Vietnam tour and left his platoon mates behind, he wanted to forget that part of his life. But things were changed. Now he hoped desperately to meet some of the men with whom he had bonded while "in country." Though none of his buddies was at the reunion, over the years, this group of veterans has become a very important part of healing for both of us. Mario has become a board member of the organization, helping plan future reunions. Amazingly, in the past few years, after more than thirty-five years of not knowing where they were, Mario has found the three people in his platoon for whom he had been searching—including the buddy who dragged him across the river.

Daniel has also attended two of the reunions with Mario—once when a teenager with plans to join the Marine Corps and once as an active-duty Marine. He valued the advice from these veterans who had actually been in combat.

Now that I am retired, I have been able to attend as well and have enjoyed the vets telling their stories, sharing their photos and, yes, sometimes crying. Though it may have been forty years since they last served, the brotherhood still remains.

Chapter Four

DANIEL

As a baby, Daniel was very good-natured and impish. He and his sister Clarissa, sixteen months his junior, were good friends.

Passionately loyal, Daniel would yell, "Shut up!" when commercials aired for a grocery store belonging to his dad's competitors. This loyalty manifested in his admiration and imitation of his father—to the point of copying his father's mannerisms, opinions, and interests. Mario was an avid soccer player and fan; Daniel was an equally avid soccer player and enthusiast. Mario was from Guatemala; Daniel told people that he was a Guatemalan. Daniel familiarized himself with maps and photos of his dad's country and listened to tapes of Guatemalan singers and marimba bands. As he got older, he and his dad exchanged salsa CDs. He even adopted his dad's penmanship style; to this day I have difficulty distinguishing between the two.

When a junior in high school, Daniel began to express the desire to become a Marine, it was an obvious emulation. I imagine most boys envision their veteran dads as heroes. Mario's military past had always fascinated him. As a pre-school child, Daniel often rummaged in Mario's closet for his solid green "utilities" (known as "fatigues" in other branches of service). He wore this clothing and his father's oversized jungle boots when he played war with other little boys. He frequently pored over every page of his father's boot camp yearbook and pilfered photos from his dad's Vietnam photo album, placing some of them next to his bed.

By the time Daniel seriously considered enlisting in the Marine Corps, the choice was a relief. As a young teenager Daniel had become associated with gang culture. Though he insists that he was never officially a member—indeed, we never witnessed any evidence of gang initiation—he found ways to associate with members of a large and well-known gang. He also ran away from time to time—usually just for a few hours. On one occasion, however, he left for several days, staying with a family he won't identify and whom we did not know.

Mario and I tried every tactic we could imagine to turn Daniel around— youth programs, the church teen group, sports, personal counseling. Even when I recently asked Daniel what he found attractive about the gang, he shrugged helplessly and admitted, "I don't really have any clue why. But they're all a bunch of losers." Fortunately, he was never arrested during these years. I give his counselor, Pat Patterson, a large part of the credit for helping Daniel through these ugly times. The Marine Corps may have satisfied lawfully what I surmise Daniel sought from gang life—being a member of a brotherhood and being part of something larger than himself. As a Marine, he would not only emulate his father but, unlike his gang association, would earn Mario's respect.

In his junior year, Daniel took the Armed Services Vocational Aptitude Battery (ASVAB) test and did quite well. His recruiter steered him towards the Delayed Enlistment Program (DEP), in which a student enlists in the Marine Corps but delays the actual entry up to a year. This permits the recruit to finish high school (or junior college) while the clock is ticking. To be considered for the DEP, a recruit must be at least seventeen years old and in his last year of high school. Additionally he/she must qualify morally (that is, have no criminal record), physically, and intellectually (a good ASVAB score as well as staying on target to graduate).

A distinct benefit of the DEP was that Daniel could request and reserve his job assignment, known as his Military Operational Specialty (MOS). This is a particular advantage when a recruit desires a popular MOS (e.g., computers) for which there are few open slots.

Another advantage of the DEP is that the recruit may choose the date on which he will begin boot camp. The time difference (up to a year) between signing the enlistment contract and the actual entry to boot camp is subtracted from the time owed later to complete his/her inactive reserve commitment. Marines are placed on an inactive reserve list for several years after serving on active duty. Contract times vary since some specialties require so much training that the commitment is lengthier. While on the inactive reserve roster, he/she can be called back to active duty in the event of national need.

As might be expected, Daniel's original choice of MOS was that of his father—0331: infantry machine gunner. The recruiter, however, convinced Daniel to choose an MOS that offered more post-Marine Corps job opportunity. So Daniel requested, and was given, the specialty of Security Force. Daniel's commitment would be for four years of active duty followed by four years of inactive reserve. However, because of his yearlong participation in the DEP, the inactive portion of his commitment would be shortened to three years.

To me, all the GI benefits, while nice, were inadequate reasons to join the service. The decision to serve deserves sober contemplation. I did not view Daniel's enlistment without some apprehension for his safety. I knew that, however improbable the prospect of war might be, ultimately my son might be needed—and must be willing—to go into combat. Having said that, who would have foreseen that the United States would soon be at war?

Because Daniel was not of legal age to sign the contract, Mario and I needed to sign permission. One June day in 2000, while I was at work, Daniel walked into my office, accompanied by a squared-away Marine wearing a precisely ironed khaki short-sleeved shirt, blue trousers with knife-edge pleats and red side stripes ("blood stripes"), shiny, spit-polished shoes, and carrying enlistment documents.

I turned to Daniel, "I'm a little nervous giving permission because with our signature your life will change. Are you sure about this step, Daniel? Now is the moment to say something if you're not ready."

"No, Mom, I'm sure. I want to be a Marine."

I believed Daniel and the Marine Corps would be good for each other, and I inked my name on the papers. Daniel would leave for boot camp on June 11 of the following year—three days after his high school graduation.

I didn't—and I don't—regret that Daniel entered the Marine Corps. Especially when there is no longer a draft to equalize the military duties to all our youth, his willingness to serve was the more exceptional. My husband, of course, thought Daniel's decision was wonderful and he was flattered that Daniel was imitating him. He did not share my concerns about Daniel taking this step. As he told Daniel and me, "Peacetime is the best time to be in the military." Any apprehension notwithstanding, we were very proud of our son.

A few weeks after signing up for the Marine Corps, Daniel passed his physical and, along with other DEP recruits, took the brief Marine Corps oath, swearing to:

> ... support and defend the Constitution against all enemies, foreign and domestic; that I will bear true faith and allegiance to the same; that I will obey the orders of the President of the United States and the orders of the officers appointed over me, according to regulations and the Uniform Code of Military Justice. So help me God.

That summer of 2000 was an exciting and enjoyable one. Knowing it would be the last carefree summer that Daniel would have, we arranged a vacation for the six of us to Washington, D.C. and New York.

A special event for Daniel and Mario was the evening program given throughout the summers by the Marines stationed at the elite Eighth and I Streets barracks. The highlight of the evening is the performance of the Silent Drill Team, which executes, without vocal cues, synchronized movements with bayoneted rifles. We also spent one evening, nostalgic for me, sitting on the Capitol steps while listening to the free band concert, just as I had done many times as a child with my family. This time we attended a performance by "The President's Own," the Marine Corps band that often plays for White House functions.

Daniel and his dad spent an afternoon at the Navy Yard's archives, poring over old transcripts of radio communications from Mario's platoon to headquarters while he was in Vietnam. When they visited the barracks at a Marine Corps base near the Naval Yard, it was with smug pleasure that Daniel flashed his new military ID, permitting them access to the PX.

We also spent a very busy few days visiting New York. We visited Ellis Island and the Statue of Liberty. One of our more poignant souvenirs is a video our son Damián took from street level of the Twin Towers at the World Trade Center in which he dizzyingly panned the length of the buildings.

Later in the summer, Daniel traveled as a member of a soccer team to Sweden and Denmark for two weeks.

In his last year of school, he spent a lot of time watching boot camp documentaries and military movies. He viewed *Full Metal Jacket* repeatedly. Another favorite was a documentary video following the progress of several Marine recruits through each week of boot camp. The latter film also helped me to understand what Daniel would experience.

He graduated from high school on June 7, 2001. On the evening of Sunday, June 10, which also happened to be Clarissa's seventeenth birthday, the recruiter came to our house in a huge van, emblazoned with Marine Corps graphics, to collect Daniel. He had no luggage; recruits may take nothing with them except their wallets and the clothes on their backs. Before heading out to Sacramento, they stopped at a local sandwich shop for dinner. In an odd coincidence, another patron recognized the recruiter as being her son's and guessed Daniel's destination. She did not know Daniel but asked him if she, as a Marine mom, could give him a goodbye hug. As it turned out, both her sons eventually became Marines, and Cheryl herself became a loyal and enthusiastic member of our support group.

After spending the night in a motel in Sacramento, Daniel was taken in the morning to the airport where he joined other Marine recruits from northern California for the flight to San Diego. Once there, they waited hours at the airport for other recruits arriving throughout the day. Following tradition, in the wee hours of the morning they were loaded onto a bus for the brief trip to the Marine Corps Recruit Depot (MCRD)—a mere few hundred yards from the airport. Once at the Marine Corps Recruit Depot, the ritual began: *"Get off my bus!"* and another generation of recruits stepped onto the famous yellow footprints. While I knew that Daniel's life would be different once he entered the Marine Corps, I did not foresee that this step would turn our lives inside out as well.

Chapter Five

BOOT CAMP

The day Daniel left for boot camp, I had a crying spell. While I never doubted I would appreciate the changes in my son that boot camp would produce, I mourned the abruptness with which he would be severed from his childhood. What if he didn't have the emotional stamina for the rigors of boot camp discipline? What if he had an injury that would prevent him from finishing?

Other than a thirty-second phone call home on the first day to confirm their arrival, recruits are permitted neither to make nor receive calls. A single brief call from a recruit to his family is sometimes allowed towards the middle of the thirteen weeks.

They are so busy from their early rising till 9:00 PM each day that recruits have scant time to write home. Sometimes they are only given a half-hour before *Taps* is sounded throughout the base. This small window of time is intended for preparation of their uniform for the next day. If there's time left over, they might write a letter home.

During the second week at MCRD, Daniel sent us a rather plaintive note:

> Dear Fam: Obviously this is hard for me to go through. The DI's [drill instructors] call us bitches and little girls and push us around. I'm not one of the recruits who they like

to pick on though so that's good. Every Sunday I get to set up the church since I was selected as lay reader. By the way, the food here is pretty good. The thing that sucks worst is having a peaceful dream in the middle of the night and waking up and seeing that I'm still here. Keep writing me back though. I will make it through. Love you all. Daniel Sagastume [I had to chuckle that Daniel added his last name—could there be another Daniel writing us from boot camp?]

Before long, there was a tone of increasing confidence in Daniel's letters. Just two weeks later, we received this letter:

Dear Fam: It's still tough, but we're getting used to it. Certain parts are hard. Putting up with the yelling and fast paced way of life is hard. The physical part isn't too bad. I've already been to the pit [an area filled with sand where more strenuous calisthenics are performed] three times. The obstacle course and rope climbing is fun. I've fought with the pugil sticks twice and won both times. One of the hard things is never being able to touch your face. After running, you can't wipe the sweat from your face, or if you have an itch, you can't scratch it.

I thought of him going through all the physical training, of having to reach down into himself for the determination to push through, even when exhausted. A few times in my own life when I am tempted to slack off, the mental image of his pressing onward still can motivate me to put forth greater effort. When ocean-kayaking that summer and my arms turned to Jell-o, I pushed on after asking myself—if Daniel is enduring worse challenges in boot camp, can I do any less?

I was not the only one inspired. Damián told me that while working as a camp counselor, he motivated his young charges during a difficult hike by using Daniel as an example of endurance.

Mario and I were out of town when Daniel was permitted a two-minute phone call halfway through boot camp. Though he spoke to Clarissa, I was crushed to have missed my only chance to speak to him in three months.

In late July he wrote:

> Dear Fam, We finally get to blouse our boots [pouf the pant legs over the tops of their boots] and leave the top buttons to our blouses unbuttoned. We had pugil sticks again the other day and I'm still undefeated. We did the fireman's carry the other day in first aid class. The drill instructors were impressed because I was able to carry someone who weighed 230 around the room. We had initial drill the other day and passed. Our platoon is finally becoming a little more disciplined. The sleep part still sucks because we bearly [sic] get any sleep because nighttime is the only time we're allowed to take a dump or iron our cammies. Tell dad that "Taps" is played every night and sometimes we're not ready in time or the drill instructors are yelling at the people who have fire watch. I told the senior drill instructor that dad was in Vietnam and when he hears "Taps" he cries and that "Taps," meant something to me because of that. So now as soon as "Taps" sound, we stand at attention and have absolute silence. So every night before I go to sleep, I think of dad. I have to go now, but keep writing. Talk to you all later. Daniel Sagastume

At the West Coast MCRD, Marine recruits relocate to Camp Pendleton, a nearby active-duty Marine base, for Phase Two. It was there that Daniel sent the most forlorn of all his letters.

> Dear Fam, Things have gotten a lot worse in the mental part. To start with the good news, the senior drill instructor wanted 4 squad leaders that showed the most leadership and he personally chose me. Then he selected a few recruits from our platoon that were good to go up to Camp

Pendleton a week earlier than the rest of the platoon. They took a few recruits from every platoon. Out of all of them, I was chosen as the guide for that week. Then it started to get bad. Whenever a recruit messes up, the guide gets taken to the pit. I was taken there everyday and sometimes 3X a day. Each pit session is 20-30 minutes so I was worn out from that. In the middle of that week I got Mom's postcard about the kayaking trip and when I read the part about her getting tired and thinking of me, I cried. Then the next day when our drill instructors weren't around, one of the sergeants from the Mess Hall (cafeteria) told me I was stupid and that I must come from stupid parents. I lost it and started yelling obscenities at him. When the drill instructor found out about it, he didn't do anything. To my relief he let it slide. Maybe he understood how much I missed my family and got so defensive. We just started growing the hair on the top of our heads and are getting ready to shoot at the rifle range. We'll be here for 4 weeks and back at San Diego for the last 2. I can't wait to see everyone when I graduate. I'll be fine even though this last week was probably my worst one yet. I have to go now, but I'll see you in September. Daniel Sagastume

During the second phase of training, recruits perform the most important skill for all Marines—rifle-qualifying. The Marine Corps demands every Marine be a rifleman. All Marines—from recruits to officers—must periodically take rifle-qualifying tests.

Recruits must attain a minimum score of 190 out of 250. If they do not achieve this standard, they must leave the group with which they have trained and bonded for the previous six weeks. Instead, they are dropped back to join a newer class of recruits, completing the remainder of their boot camp training with the new group.

Dear Fam, Sorry, but I've been busy lately. We had qual-day at the rifle range. I was stressed because the day before,

I shot 174 out of a necessary 190 to pass. If you don't pass, they drop you [back] 2 weeks. I was already thinking about what I would say during the phone call home to let you know I wasn't graduating September 7, but on qual-day I started hitting bulls-eyes and came [within] 3 points of Expert. I am a rifle Sharpshooter. It's weird to think that we're on field week and the Monday after you get this letter, I will be on the Crucible and back down to San Diego for the last 2 weeks to prepare for Graduation and then home. When you all come here there will be a D.I. dinner. Tell dad to bring a lot of money to buy my drill instructor a round of beers. I know you all hate <u>fast food,</u> but I want a hamburger when I get out of here. Bring my CDs too. I miss all those things.... Bring my money stash so I can buy my dress blues. I gotta go, but I love you all. I'll be home soon. Bye! Daniel Sagastume

During the weeks spent at Camp Pendleton Daniel took many long and rigorous hikes while wearing full gear and carrying heavy packs. During Field Training week recruits participated in day and night live-ammunition exercises. Live-fire training exposes recruits to the chaos and din of actual battle (which cannot be duplicated with "dummy" ammunition). Becoming accustomed to the din and confusion of battle is thought to diminish the chances of freezing up psychologically during combat. Daniel confided that Field Week was the most difficult of all the weeks of boot camp.

The ultimate challenge in Phase Two is the Crucible, which was added to the training matrix in 1996. Though somewhat altered now, during Daniel's time the Crucible consisted of a fifty-four hour period during which teams of recruits complete a forty-mile hike under food- and sleep-deprived conditions and are challenged by combat assault courses, a problem-solving reaction course, and team-building exercises.

Daniel's last letter from boot camp was written just before going on the Crucible:

Sorry for not writing lately. I've gotten 5 hours of sleep a night during field week. Every night we would hike and do night infiltration courses and ambushes. Now it's the Crucible. We will get even less sleep and little food for 3 days. Just a few more weeks here. I finished the gas chambers. That was the biggest mental test. Your skin burns, you can't breathe, and you start to go crazy. You can't think about anything but thinking you're going to die. When you get out though, you feel good. We did night fire with tracers. It felt like we were Jedis from Star wars, seeing the fire shoot at that speed.

Daniel sent a list of food that he wanted me to bring to graduation: a bag of Reese's, M&Ms, and a chocolate fudge cake with sliced bananas on top. He looked forward to eating pizza and going to Taco Bell and Subway, but what he wanted first was a hamburger.

With a month to go, Daniel was bubbling with thoughts of graduation. He looked forward to seeing his family at the ceremonies and fantasized about watching Monday night football with his brother Mario when he got home.

In Phase Three, boot camp training is ramped down. The last martial arts skills are taught in this phase. Physical Fitness Training (PFT) as well as the recruits' skills rappelling down a tall concrete tower are tested during this time. Recruits are fitted for the duty uniforms they will wear after graduation; they fill out forms, including power of attorney and wills; and receive travel instructions for their next training station. Since the drill instructors compete among themselves to have the best marching platoon during the graduation ceremony, the recruits spend much time perfecting their marching precision.

After thirteen weeks I couldn't wait to wrap my arms around my boy again. I chided myself that I'd better stop thinking of him as a "boy." Completing Marine Corps boot camp definitely earned him the right to be called a man.

To me, though, he would always be Daniel, my youngest son. Daniel with the impish grin. The little boy who worried that someone else might eat that last piece of cake. He was still the little five-year-old who was so fiercely loyal to the Sacramento Kings during their hapless seasons that he burst into tears of frustration when the team lost yet again. Only now, his loyalty was focused on the Marine Corps.

With much excitement, Mario, Clarissa, and I drove to San Diego the day after Labor Day. Daniel's brothers would arrive the following day for the graduation, as would other relatives, including Mario's father, who, thirty-five years before, had come to MCRD for Mario's boot camp graduation.

In 2001, graduation week festivities were kicked off by a Wednesday dinner for the recruits' families. Then we assembled on the lawn, and before long, we heard the crescendo of male voices chanting cadence. In the deepening twilight, phalanxes of Marine recruits marched in formation by platoons, toward us. As they neared, I could see that the sleeves of their camouflage shirts were rolled neatly at mid-biceps and their eight-point "covers" (caps) crisply ironed. At the head of each platoon a recruit held an identifying "guidon" (a pennant-shaped flag). Daniel's platoon was 2084.

The crowd erupted in shrieks. The families could barely endure waiting as Marine recruits stood in formation and, eyes fixed straight ahead, sang the *Marine Corps Hymn*—all three verses. Only then were they dismissed.

Clarissa squealed when she saw Daniel and ran to him. Mario grabbed him in a bear hug, his eyes moist with pride. I waited my turn, all the while sobbing with relief.

We families had our Marines to ourselves for only an hour, so recruits and families excitedly and rapidly exchanged news of the previous thirteen weeks. Dusk became nighttime; all too soon the recruits were called to formation and marched back to the barracks. Fulfilling Daniel's request, Mario and I bought Daniel's drill instructors a few rounds of beer.

Families arrived on the grounds of MCRD the next morning to watch their recruits take their last "moto" run, or motivational training run. Recruits dressed in olive drab shorts and shirts shot off to the rhythm of cadence while the "honor man" from each platoon ran with the guidon. Recruits are supposed to ignore family members that are, in fact, only feet away, but Clarissa and I both tried to break Daniel's game face by whooping, calling his name, and sounding our family's signature whistle. We were rewarded by the merest trace of a smile at the corners of Daniel's mouth before he sprinted from our sight.

We saw him later that morning for the ceremony at which recruits received the pin depicting the emblem of the Marine Corps—the Eagle, Globe, and Anchor—which would be worn on their uniforms from that point onward.

The recruits, wearing olive trousers, short-sleeved khaki blouses, and garrison caps (the flat "fore and aft" caps) sported the so-called "high and tight" haircut (modified from the severe recruit crew cut) that would be required from now on. They were so handsome and proud as they solemnly marched in step. After some remarks by the battalion commander, the drill instructors, uniformed similarly to the recruits but with polished swords at their hips, presented each recruit with his pin.

Though some were seventeen years old, the average age of the five hundred and fifty new Marines was eighteen. These sober young faces grimaced into stoic expressions. For me the moment was bittersweet. These men, so proud of their accomplishment and so eager in their desire to defend our country, had just made such a formidable commitment that my heart began to be troubled by a barely-perceptible heaviness.

The new Marines had received their pins, but they wouldn't actually graduate from boot camp until the ceremony the following day. They were restricted to the grounds of MCRD, but could spend the next several hours with their families. I remember being so proud to stroll around MCRD on the arm of my handsome Marine son.

The Friday morning of graduation, the hot sun seared my arms as I climbed the risers facing the parade grounds. The military band played John Philip Souza marches, and I watched the ceremony, my emotions tumbling upon each other as if they were towels in a dryer.

My son's rite of passage signaled my own. It would now be his generation to whom the exciting milestone events would happen.

"All the exciting things are behind us," I protested to Mario. "Other than grandchildren and retirement, what other milestone is left for us except dying?"

I wasn't devastated, but it did put me on notice that we were aging. Mario's Vietnam era Marines would now be the "old guys"; their military roles now the stuff of history. In front of us were The New Warriors.

After meeting and congratulating the graduates, we packed Daniel's sea bag in our van and drove to a nearby pizza parlor for a quick celebration with Mario's family (unfortunately for Daniel, that hamburger would have to wait).

My vague sense of impending doom began to expand, confusing me. As our family of six traveled on the long ride home, I leaned my head against the car window, hoping to conceal my freely flowing tears.

Indeed, Daniel's boot camp graduation was the first of four events during Daniel's service that turned my world upside down.

When we were by ourselves, Mario asked, "What's wrong with you?"

"I don't understand it," I began. "I'm so proud of Daniel and of all these new Marines, but all I could think of is that they have just offered to put their lives down for all of us." My voice quivered.

"They are all someone's babies. They made the promise, but they don't know what they've done. They're too young to understand the full magnitude of this commitment."

Throughout the days that followed I tried to come to grips with knowing that my son—and all those sons—might have to go into harm's way. Upon my return home, I wrote in my diary:

> This isn't about letting him go physically. Rather, this is a spiritual challenge. I must say "yes" in my heart to Daniel's choices in life—no matter the outcome.

> But what if he makes the ultimate sacrifice? I keep reminding myself that he is God's child, not mine. Nonetheless, my sadness for all these young men who risk their lives is so profound that I puddle up multiple times a day. I know we're not at war, yet here I am neurotically grieving as if these guys were going off to battle. What is wrong with me? Why am I so emotional? It's out of proportion to the situation. I feel totally crazy!

Over the next few days, though it didn't make sense to me, I had the strong feeling that I needed to work through this issue while there was time. If I were able to reconcile myself to this, I figured I'd be able to cope better should the world situation change and my son have to go to war.

I am not someone who cries easily or often. In fact, I can go years without crying. But in the days after Daniel's boot camp graduation, I found that I was having short though frequent meltdowns—as often as ten to twenty times a day.

When I returned to work the Monday after graduation, I had trouble even describing the ceremonies without choking up. I told a co-worker that I was so sad thinking of those men putting their very young lives on the line. She responded, "I can't understand why you're so sad. It's not as if we were at war."

"I realize that. But the world can change just like *that*!" I snapped my fingers sharply.

At home my family was bewildered by my lachrymose behavior. Though I tried to hide my crying episodes from Daniel, he rolled his eyes at me, "Mom, cut it out!" This dramatic excess was not in character for me, and I was exhausted by it.

On Monday evening, September 10, as I left a meeting, I stood in the parking lot and gazed at the stars glittering in the night sky, wondering for the millionth time, "What is the matter with me?" My co-worker was right. The current world situation didn't warrant such excess emotion.

In a sudden flash of intuition, I realized that my reaction wasn't sadness; it was a more profound emotion—mourning. What a relief to name the emotion appropriately. That provided clarity: I had been mourning deeply— albeit a bit dramatically. What I didn't understand was "why?" I looked at the heavens as an intuitive thought formed in my head. "Could I possibly be mourning for something that hasn't happened yet? Inexplicably, the notion that I was grieving for something still "out there" in the future suddenly felt right—even if it seemed goofy.

The second of the four life-changing events during Daniel's enlistment occurred the following morning.

Chapter Six

SEPTEMBER 11, 2001

Tuesdays were my days off. I was looking forward to this Tuesday to kick back after the turmoil of the graduation. My plan was to go running and later take Daniel out to lunch, for a little mother-son time. That morning I was indulging myself with the luxury of sleeping in. Mario, habitually an early riser, was bustling in the kitchen. A vague awareness of his rustling and the bold aroma of brewing espresso inserted itself into my dreams.

Just before 6:00 AM, I jerked awake as Mario exploded through the bedroom door, stomped across the room to the television, and punched the "power" button. His lips pursed in a scowl, his voice crackled with fury.

"An airplane just flew into one of the World Trade Center's towers!"

I nestled under the covers a little deeper; I wasn't ready to awaken yet. I lazily stretched my toes. I kept my eyes closed for a few seconds longer. Finally, I turned toward the screen, then stared stupidly at the television as the on-air commentators guessed the numbers of individuals inside the tower and discussed the feasibility of their rescue by helicopter.

Though Mario had grasped the implication of this event as soon as the first plane struck the tower, I was still uncomprehending. Had there been some terrible accident? Only when the other plane approached the second tower, did all illusions evaporate.

I bolted out of bed, my heart jackhammering as I watched the second plane hit. In horror, I saw the towers implode, as a vivid image of three thousand occupants shrieking in terror played out in my head.

I could feel hot spurts of adrenalin surge through my abdomen. My hands trembled. There was no doubt now; I had just witnessed *our* generation's Pearl Harbor. This was a deliberate act of war. But by whom?

Fear for all of us gushed through my body, followed by terror for Daniel, whose life, I realized, would be directly affected by this act. Certain that there would be a military response, I realized his time in the Marine Corps would now be the longest four years of my life.

Daniel was asleep in the bedroom next to ours. As I did when he was a baby, I now crept into his room for a few minutes to reassure myself that he was there, to listen to his slow, even breaths. I watched him sleep for a bit, placing my head against the side of his mattress. Before long, thoughts of him going to war made me sob loudly enough that he awoke.

Daniel's recruiter called later that morning to verify his whereabouts and his contact information. I feared this might mean he would have to immediately report to his next training station, but since air travel was placed in a lockdown for the rest of the week, that didn't happen.

The confusion of facts and rumors and not knowing whether to expect more attacks in the next few hours or days ratcheted up my anxiety to a virtually unbearable level.

I tried to resume some routine that day, but it was impossible. I still took Daniel out to lunch, but weak attempts on my part to hold a conversation were futile. All talk inevitably reverted to the events of the day. I could do little more than stare, as if in a mute trance, at the news on the sports bar television.

That night, I slept fitfully while the vision of a plane hitting the twin towers repeated itself continuously in my dreams. I also had a dream that continued to disturb me for years afterward.

Daniel and a squad of Marines were patrolling in an unknown foreign country, using the protective cover of a copse of trees. As the other Marines moved out, they unwittingly left Daniel behind in a small hollow between hills. The voices of the others faded as they moved farther away and the silence that remained vibrated with eeriness. In my dream it isn't clear whether Daniel was injured, but I saw him lying on his back, watching the clouds scud across the sky. The intense panic I felt as Daniel was left behind with the enemy audibly nearby made me awaken with a start. This dream creeped me out so badly I could not go back to sleep for hours afterward. I was afraid the dream was somehow an omen.

From my journal:

> My anxiety has the upper hand.…I feel panic at the thought of losing Daniel—and I feel that he [may be killed]. I can't tell whether [this is] intuition or anxious rumination about the danger. If I knew it was anxiety I could try to dismantle it, but I don't know.

Indeed, the heavy sense of foreboding that the dream might be a premonition hovered around my consciousness the entire four years Daniel was in the service.

Sometime shortly after the attacks, First Lady Laura Bush spoke on television. She was so serene; how did she do that? I envied her apparent composure! I remember saying during this period that I wished I could be calm like Laura Bush. Though I uttered that tongue-in-cheek, I longed for a similar calm; I sorely needed comforting.

During the weeks that followed, I had to make an active effort to calm myself. A September 22 entry in my journal addressed this:

> My emotions seesaw daily and with each news bulletin that I feverishly listen for. Even upon awakening, I panic that something has happened while I slept. Yet, I am afraid to turn on the news because, as long as I don't know it yet, I don't have to deal with it.

Eventually over the weeks and years, I learned to ration the news to only top-of-the-hour news briefs and a single detailed news report after work. This helped me to minimize runaway anxiety. I learned to adopt some self-nurturing practices to lower my agitation: I played CDs of relaxing music at work to soothe me, which I especially appreciated when the news day was bad. I placed landscape photos in my office; the beauty of these delighted my soul. I occasionally bought myself flowers. I filled my office and my sitting room at home with potpourri. This treat to my senses provided restorative refuge and fostered a temporary feeling of well-being.

Deliberately deciding to substitute a different emotion for fear, I decided to play up patriotic pride. My vast wardrobe of Marine shirts and the bumper stickers on my car were more about boosting my own morale than about bragging to others.

As much as I am ashamed to admit it, the terrorists did achieve their goal: they had intimidated me and their actions changed my life forever. My trust in the safety and the reliable predictability of my world vanished. September 11 signaled not only a change in the kind of military experience Daniel would have, it changed my personal priorities and rearranged my thinking. It also affected me in ways the terrorists did not intend.

I knew I had become lazy about self-discipline. I like my creature comforts, but now seemed to be an appropriate time to toughen up. If self-discipline elicited strength of character, then I decided to develop this virtue and learn to practice some rudimentary self-denial.

The events of 9/11 gave all of us an awareness of our mortality. This tragic event underscored for me that time was precious and finite. I now wished to prune my life and spend time on activities that were important to me, and drop those which seemed frivolous of my time.

A desire to live a more authentic life became urgent after September 11. For the first time, I began to find my voice, urging myself to be more assertive about my needs and worry less about others' reactions. I was emboldened to speak more frankly and reminded myself to "let the chips fall where they may."

That fateful day also affected my perspective on the world. I abhor personal violence and am acutely uncomfortable when in the presence of angry people. When my children were young I was not able to wink at their backyard brawls with each other. Though my sons took Tae Kwon Do, I found martial arts distasteful for me; I could not bear to even mimic the martial arts moves occasionally used in my aerobics classes. When I once glimpsed the cold gray metal of the revolver in an officer's holster, I found it ominously chilling. My husband spoke from time to time of wanting to own a gun just for safety reasons, but I had been adamant that there be no weapons in our house. With all this reluctance toward any kind of violence, I was surprised to realize that I felt the need for a military response to the acts of terrorism on September 11.

In my journal I noted that:

> I don't feel anger—just grief. As the second plane came into the tower, it seemed immediately clear that this is not negotiable. This is an act of war, and we can't *not* respond. I have no desire to exact revenge. But this is *evil*. It must not be permitted to thrive.... We must act, not talk. There is no time to lose; more innocent lives are at stake. Having said all this, I am abject at sending Daniel into harm's way. Yet, why should my son's life be spared rather than some other mother's? I realize that much of my reaction has been selfish—how all of this affects my son and me. Yet, I don't want Afghan women to lose their sons either.... How do you pray enough in this situation?... I can't think how to solve this problem. Guerilla warfare might flush out bin-Laden, but what good is an air strike—unless it is a known terrorist headquarters? How is talking helpful? Bin-Laden hasn't asked for negotiation. Besides, he isn't making a point to get us to change our foreign policy. Rather, his aim is to destroy us.

The attack absolutely enraged Mario. He wanted to *do* something. He wanted to be included in our country's effort to catch the perpetrators. He was indignant that he was considered "too old" to go and fight for his country again. He couldn't bear being cut out of the action. The country needed warriors, and he felt he still had something to offer. Over the next several months he made futile efforts (and indeed many of his veteran friends were doing the same thing) to find some venue in which his knowledge could benefit those currently serving in the Marine Corps. Thus began four years of frustration as he watched younger men do battle when he felt that he still possessed a lot of hard-won combat wisdom that would go untapped.

All too soon, Daniel's ten-day leave came to an end. He was to report to Camp Pendleton for further training at the School of Infantry (SOI) on September 18. Air travel had resumed but travelers were afraid to get on airplanes. I was fearful of Daniel's going even on this one-hour flight. With effort, I soothed myself with the affirmation that it was highly unlikely that any American would ever again allow someone to overtake a plane.

He had been instructed, for safety reasons, not to wear his military uniform when traveling and was dressed in shorts, a shirt, and athletic shoes. With his hair trimmed in the regulation "high and tight" and his uniforms in a garment bag with a large Marine Corps emblem on it, his status was hardly a well-kept secret. Someone in the check-in line even said "thank you for serving" to him.

We're all quite used to the limitations of airport security now, but I was disappointed that the new, enhanced measures—unveiled just that week—were not uniformly applied. In spite of the fact that he had presented his military I.D. as his form of identification, Daniel was the only traveler singled out for a more thorough search. This included removing items from his luggage and inspecting all his dress and camouflage uniforms as well as his field boots. I am not sure why Daniel was selected for further screening unless it was due to his one-way ticket (though several other new Marines reporting to SOI and taking the same one-way flight had not been inspected) or the fact that he had a darker complexion (possibly Middle Eastern-looking). Who knows? Daniel was unruffled by the security process; Mario, however, was furious and kept muttering scornful comments. I hissed to him not to be so testy. After all, these were now tense times. The airline employees had to be nervous and the passengers equally anxious. Belligerent comments wouldn't help the stress level.

With the events of the previous week, I didn't know if the Marine Corps would keep their original training plan for Daniel, or if, now that there was a wartime emergency, the contract for his MOS would be voided. We were afraid Daniel might be sent to war immediately upon completion of his infantry training, as Mario had been. We didn't know whether we were going to see Daniel again before he went off to a war that surely was to come.

I had promised myself that I wouldn't cry when it was time to say goodbye. But when Daniel had a hard time saying good-bye too, Mario and

I both started to cry. Daniel has since told us that particular good-bye was one of the most difficult ones he has ever experienced.

Upon our return, we were confronted by Daniel's belongings, which were strewn around our house. I had mixed feelings about altering his bedroom, but to leave it unchanged was an equally painful reminder of his absence. I knew that from now on Daniel would not be staying in our home except for brief visits, and he would never belong in the same way he had for the previous eighteen years. Since we were desperate for additional space, we decided to turn Daniel's room into an office for Mario. Mario's eyes filled with tears whenever he thought about Daniel no longer living in this bedroom.

On the day of his departure we hung a Marine Corps flag in front of our house. That flag, as well as an American flag, has remained ever since to honor Daniel and Mario and their choice to serve.

I wondered how I would survive the next four years. I wondered how other families with children in the military coped. I know this sounds terribly naïve, but I really thought that somehow military families must be different; that they had some unusual level of confidence—the right stuff—that allowed them to be immune to worry.

On the other hand, I didn't feel brave at all; I was scared. All right, I was terrified. So it was with more bravado than bravery, a kind of whistling through the graveyard, that I approached the next few months.

I wanted a mentor in this process. If *I* was anxious, perhaps there were other military families in the community who were feeling the same way in these uncertain times. Since combat seemed inevitable, it was quite possible that in the coming months some of the military sons and daughters in our community might be injured or killed. I reasoned that we military families needed to make connections with each other now. Then, in the event of a tragedy, there would already be a network of people available to comfort and assist. Over the years I have come to feel that, just as our service people learn that they are part of a team that takes care of one another, it is up to us, the military family members, to take care of each other. I believe that the morale of our troops is indirectly benefited by the knowledge that their families are being looked after.

I first checked to see if the Marine recruiter knew of a local support group I could join and was dismayed to learn no such group existed. I don't remember precisely how it evolved, but I think my friend Janet suggested I start a group myself. I rejected that idea at first. I wasn't trained to lead a group. Why, I didn't even know any other parents of Marines. Moreover, I didn't want to entrap myself with anything that might require a lot of time.

But I began to regret denying myself the very thing I wanted merely because I was afraid to challenge myself. And hadn't communication techniques been drilled in my head in nursing school? Didn't my daily job as a nurse practitioner involve using those communication techniques to facilitate a patient's expression of his true concerns? My desire to connect with other military parents outweighed my performance anxiety. I decided that I could do this. I *would* do this.

Though I didn't know any Marine parents, I knew quite a few people whose sons were in the Navy, and I invited them to the new support group. Janet provided me with contact information for two local Marine families she knew. I also asked the Marine recruiter to give my name and phone number to those he thought would be interested in taking part in a support group. He actually was very helpful in obtaining several referrals. Some guests invited others to the first meeting. One stranger was invited when it was noted that her car had a "Navy Mom" bumper sticker.

My guest list was growing. I decided not to put an announcement for the first meeting in the newspaper lest too many people come, which would limit intimacy in the group. There have been several changes in our group's name over the years. Formerly the Marine-Navy Family Support Group, it is now the Military Family Support Group. Our members include families from all branches of service.

I scheduled the first meeting for the evening of Tuesday, October 2, in our home. I had no way of knowing how many persons would show up; it might be two, or fifty-two. My high school daughter thought the whole idea was "lame." I sure hoped the parents didn't feel that way too. I didn't plan any agenda for the gathering except for us to meet each other. I had butterflies in my stomach that day, worrying that the meeting would be a fiasco, and I repeatedly wondered why I had put myself in this position. I set my dining room table with all kinds of snacks and light beverages, arranged chairs around in a circle in my living room, and waited.

To my surprise, twenty people showed up. None had a female loved one in the military, which remained true for almost a decade. Though our members have been predominantly parents (Mario wasn't the only dad who attended), we have also had girlfriends, sisters, wives, and grandparents.

I still am able to recall which people sat in which seat as they described their child's situation at that first meeting.

One mother said her son was presumed now to be in Afghanistan in the capacity of Marine sniper. Imagine how surprised she was to learn that she was sitting right next to a mother whose son was also a Marine sniper presumed to be in Afghanistan. One Marine mom had spent the day of September 11 anxiously waiting for word about her sister, who, as a United Air Lines stewardess, frequently flew the same routes that the hijackers had chosen. This same guest had also been frightened for a niece who lived near the World Trade Center Towers. Though her relatives had in fact been unharmed, this tragedy made her feel especially vulnerable.

The group agreed to meet once a month. The format for future meetings was that, in round-robin fashion, each attendee would bring the group up to date about their military person. I sensed the political preferences among the group's members were quite varied. Accordingly, politics was a forbidden topic; I wanted each member to feel the meetings were a place of refuge rather than more stress. Over the years there have been a few times when conversations have briefly overstepped the boundaries. Nonetheless, in the main, we have avoided political discussion and maintain a warm congeniality. In fact, one of the most ardent enthusiasts of the group's value is a member who joined our group in January of 2003. She was an active anti-war protestor whose son was about to be deployed to Iraq. She was terrified for him and, initially, leery that we might all be, as she said, "flag-wavers." As she discovered, we were not interested in her politics. What was important was that, like everyone else in the group, she had a loved one in the service and needed our support.

The majority of persons at that first meeting returned to attend other meetings. The "charter members" formed a core of reliably regular attendees and the formation of this group came to be a most fortuitous event for many of us over the years. Many of us discovered, whether at work or other arenas of our lives, no one else was in the same situation.

To those who have scornfully objected, as my mother did, "Didn't you know what you were in for when Daniel signed up?" the answer is, "Of course I did." But *I* did not enlist; my service is involuntary. That is not to say that Mario and I opposed Daniel's decision; rather, we had no choice in the matter. Our role was to accept his life choice, adapt to it, and support him. When we military families offer our love and emotional support—waiting and worrying while our loved ones fulfill their duties—we also are in service to our country.

I was proud of my son's choice to serve. Trying to make peace with the possible consequences of that decision is something different altogether. Throughout Daniel's entire active-duty commitment, I tried to accept the reality that my son could die in war. Without a doubt, I would be devastated if my child was killed. I don't wish to presume I would know how I would feel if my child were to die, but I certainly rehearsed such a scenario many, many times during those four years. Knowing that he had chosen this path in life, and that serving one's country is a lofty aspiration, gave me some peace. I know death can also come unexpectedly to a non-military child. But the military family's situation is unique in that during the time the child serves—particularly in wartime—parents face the *constant* threat that their child might be killed. Should a child be killed in combat, a parent's grief is exacerbated by the realization that the child's death wasn't an aberration of nature. Rather, someone intended him to die—in fact, desired his family's anguish. Perhaps the perpetrator hoped families' morale and that of their countrymen would falter with the deaths of our troops.

Because military service is not an equal obligation, as it is during a draft, fewer people understand what the military family copes with. Our support group became an important part of our lives. I learned so much from listening to others. Since Marines could expect to deploy at least once on a Navy ship, I was interested to learn from the sailors' parents. Of special interest were the stories from one couple whose son served on an aircraft carrier in the Persian Gulf and was directly involved in the early efforts against the Taliban.

I furtively watched others in the group—especially those whose sons were already in Afghanistan—to see how these parents managed. I learned how to cope better myself by watching the dignified courage these parents modeled. I soon learned that we all were afraid for our sons and military families weren't made of different stuff after all.

I wanted the group members to feel as if we were a family. I e-mailed members between meetings and I also phoned people who contacted me but never came to meetings. This last group seemed reassured that, should they eventually feel the need, our group was available.

It was important to me to make the effort to memorize the details of each member's situation: their loved one's MOS, to know which member's child was due home on leave, which parent hadn't heard yet from their son, etc. I think establishing this group may have been one of the things I was put on earth to do, but I benefited from it as much as anyone else did. I couldn't have managed during Daniel's eventual deployment to Iraq without the support and love of these wonderful people. After each meeting I felt my spirits uplifted by the love we gave each other.

Chapter Seven

SCHOOL OF INFANTRY (SOI)

Camp Pendleton is a sprawling base that covers approximately 200 square miles of terrain between the coastal towns of San Clemente and Oceanside in California. Sixty thousand military and civilian personnel live on the base. It is the home of the West Coast's Marine Corps School of Infantry.

All Marines have some sort of infantry training, the length of which is determined by their MOS. Since Daniel's MOS was 0311—Infantry—his training was of longer duration. In 2001, training lasted approximately eight weeks. In recent years, infantry training time has been altered to accommodate the complex knowledge needed in today's War on Terror. Marines now have more training in dealing with IED's (the notorious Improvised Explosive Devices that have maimed and killed so many of our military men and women in Iraq and Afghanistan), as well as patrolling and convoy operations.

When Daniel attended SOI, training covered warfare systems; tactics; weapons systems and the operation of basic weapons (such as machine guns and grenade launchers), as well as specialized weapons like the Squad Automatic Weapon (SAW); the combination of such weapons as mortars, machine guns, anti-tank weapons; both day and nighttime land navigation; stealth; and urban warfare. There was more extensive training in field skills, martial arts, and, of course, more physical training.

Several days after he arrived at SOI, Daniel called to say that it would be a few weeks yet before a new infantry training class would start. In the meantime, he and the other new Marines were assigned to guard posts around the base. In the jittery weeks following 9/11, securing the base from terrorist incursion was serious business. Nonetheless, nighttime guard duty seemed very eerie and melancholic to him. He struggled to invent mental games that would help him stay awake when he was on post by himself in the hours before dawn. Even now, when Daniel recalls his weeks on guard duty at SOI, he considers them to be some of the most difficult and dispiriting.

At the end of September we received a woeful note from Daniel written on a page torn from a small memo pad:

> Dear Fam, I knew it would be hard to leave [home to go to SOI], but I'm more homesick now than I was in boot camp. I want you two, Mom and Dad, to visit me the first weekend I have off. I miss you both so much.... In case you're wondering what we're doing now, we're guards for the base, which is serious. We have live rounds and are told to use them if necessary, especially with the recent events that have occurred. I'm off duty right now so I'm writing. Will be a guard for a few weeks until we start actual SOI training.... I love you. Bye. Daniel.

On the first weekend in October, we made the ten-hour drive to Camp Pendleton, arriving at about four in the afternoon on Friday. Being familiar with the base, Mario had no trouble locating Daniel's barracks. Daniel's group had been told they would be given liberty by late afternoon, but the instructors kept them well beyond that time ordering them to repeatedly clean their weapons.

Meanwhile, we waited at the little on-base pizza parlor down the street from SOI, expecting Daniel to show up momentarily so we could all eat together. And we waited. And we waited. Finally, at about 9:00 PM, the Marines in Daniel's platoon were released for their liberty. However, instead of being able to go off base to eat at a restaurant or to stay at the motel with us, Daniel's group was now restricted to the base. I was thrilled to see him, but disappointed that we couldn't take him out for a steak dinner or anything else festive.

While we had been waiting for Daniel at the pizza parlor, I found myself in a kind of culture shock. No doubt about it: I had definitely stepped into male territory. Marines were everywhere. Camouflage uniforms, desert field boots, and floppy-brimmed boonie hats were the dress of the majority. Not the roar of large seven-ton trucks, the jeeps rumbling down the road, or the loud whipping of blades from Marine helicopters overhead warranted as much as a glance from them. Though I have been to Camp Pendleton a number of times since, each time I still find the sudden relocation to this alien, masculine world a little disorienting.

When I saw that evening just how many Marines were at that base, their sheer numbers reassured me. I considered how many other Marines were stationed at other large bases—not to mention the number of persons serving in other branches of service—and I was comforted to realize that so many men and women were available and willing to protect us.

During the next afternoon, we listened to a CD of Loggins and Messina Daniel had asked us to bring, as we three drove around the base. He particularly liked the tracks, *Danny's Song* and the *House at Pooh Corner*. These were tunes that Mario sang while he played his guitar when our children were young. Daniel became quiet while Mario and I sang along to *House at Pooh Corner*. Thinking that perhaps he had nodded off, I flipped the mirror on my sun visor to check on him in the back seat. He was looking pensively out his side window, his eyes moist. Could Daniel have instinctively been trying to recapture his childhood, a time when he and his world were safe? Indeed, soon enough, as a Marine he would shoulder some of the responsibility for the world's safety.

An inconvenient drawback to Daniel's confinement to the base was that there was no good place for us to sit and relax together or to talk. The ambiance of the restaurants on base was not conducive to intimate conversation.

Which brings me to an observation: There seemed to be a paucity of places to eat on base, other than fast food franchises, and few, if any, "healthy food" establishments. For those Marines who did not have cars or for those whose training schedules caused them to miss chow time, fast food establishments on base were the only alternative. This seemed peculiarly counter-productive for an organization that prizes physical fitness.

Mario and I ended up getting sandwiches and taking them to a small park on base so we could picnic. After lunch Daniel lay down on the blanket and, as we witnessed many times throughout the visit, within moments, was asleep.

By dinnertime one of the few places on base where we could eat together in the evening with relative privacy was the bowling alley. We ordered a meal of hamburgers, French fries, and Krispy Kreme donuts at the concession counter. (Talk about unhealthy food choices!)

As we ate, Mario and Daniel had the most amazingly wide-ranging conversation that lasted almost two hours.

"I manage to get along with most people," Daniel said, "which has helped when I've had to be a leader."

Mario countered, "Yeah, Mijo ['my son' in Spanish]. A lot of guys seem to think you have to be a jerk when you lead people, but it's not necessary to be mean or rude. I find that if you are polite when asking for something, people usually cooperate."

"Dad, how did you handle being away from all your family for the thirteen months you were in Vietnam?"

"I don't really remember exactly what I did. I know I missed my family, but the buddies in the field with you become your family. And you're so busy and you're tired when you're not busy. I don't remember what I did; I just got through it. And you will too."

They discussed tips for staying awake while on guard duty.

Then Daniel asked, "Did you have to kill anyone, Dad? What is it like to kill someone? How do you make yourself do that?"

"There was a time that several of us shot at the enemy. I don't know which of us shot the bullet that killed him, but it could have been me. You just have to realize that the enemy will kill you if you don't kill him first. I didn't take any pleasure in killing anyone. It's what I had to do to survive.

"Sometimes you find that you hate anyone from that country because you're angry at what they did to your friends. That anger may stay with you long after you get back. You can't really help how you feel."

"I still have trouble with my feelings. I don't know if you've noticed it: sometimes I'm elaborately polite to people from Vietnam. That's because I know that it isn't okay to act on those irrational feelings. I'm carefully polite because I want to be sure I don't act rudely."

I was glad Daniel was able to unburden himself to his father and cheered to think his dad would be there for him again when Daniel would be combat-seasoned himself. Mario looked forward to being available to help Daniel negotiate psychological fallout after he returned from war and avoid the mistakes he himself had made by not talking about his experiences or dealing with his PTSD sooner.

As rewarding as it was to listen to their personal exchange, my heart was heavy. Was this precious time being given to us so Daniel's relationship with his dad could deepen? Was it given to us to allow us a chance to have special memories to reflect on later, should something happen to Daniel? This was my dilemma then and throughout the next four years: Was I just being neurotic, or was I being intuitive?

Sunday morning while we were in one of the stores on base, the radio announced that the United States had initiated the bombing of specific targets in Afghanistan. Though I knew a response had been inevitable—indeed necessary—I was frightened now that the conflict had begun. I knew we were now committed to a course that would begin to change world dynamics. I also wondered what kind of reprisals there might be against us for this action.

Since Mario and I had to be at work on Monday morning, we left Camp Pendleton on Sunday afternoon for the ten-hour drive back. Daniel asked us to come see him again the following weekend when he anticipated an off-base liberty, and we agreed.

It had been great to see and hug Daniel. He hadn't seemed depressed, merely appropriately sober. I sensed he had wanted the reassurance of our presence to boost his own spirits. I hoped it had.

On the trip home, we were silent with our private melancholy. It was painful to leave Daniel behind to train for war. With all that had happened only three and a half weeks before, our hearts were raw.

Stopping for dinner, we were lost in grief as we robotically gnawed our meal. When I glanced over at Mario, his eyes welled with tears. I reached over to pat his arm, just as tears escaped.

"I can't help it. I'm a f—g basket case! I miss my buddy already," he moaned, his face crumpling. We must have been an odd sight sitting at a center table, with tears dribbling down our cheeks and plopping onto our food. We comforted ourselves with the realization that at least we would see Daniel soon.

The following Friday after work, we drove to Camp Pendleton again, arriving at 2:00 AM at our motel. Four hours later Daniel called for us to pick him up.

Daniel's class had been given a liberty for the weekend, but only a "Cinderella liberty." That meant that he could go off base, but had to be back on base from midnight to 6:00 AM. On Saturday evening the three of us drove to San Diego. The Air Force Academy's soccer team was in town for a game, and we visited Mario's brother Louie (who was the head coach) and his nephew Marcus (who played midfield for the team). Unfortunately we couldn't go to the evening game because there wasn't enough time to get back to Camp Pendleton before the midnight curfew.

On Sunday, the three of us again traveled the forty miles to San Diego. After eating breakfast with Daniel's uncle and cousin before they flew back to Colorado, we went to Coronado Island. We thought it would be nice to spend some time with Daniel at the beach, but, instead, we watched Daniel sleep soundly on the sand as people squealed, threw Frisbees, and children played around him. We wondered: how can people seem carefree at a time when it seemed that the world was spinning out of control? Would this very island, with its Navy base, be targeted? Would someone, acting out of hate, permanently alter our personal lives? Would this new action in Afghanistan change the world in some definable way?

As we drove Daniel back to base before driving home, I told him that as much as we wanted to see him, we were too old and too weary to manage another long trip the following weekend. Wouldn't you know, the very next weekend he was given liberty—a true liberty weekend with no restrictions.

Daniel completed SOI on Thursday, November 1, 2001, and was scheduled to travel to Virginia to begin Security Force School for more training in his MOS. I had hoped he would be able to fly home for the weekend before traveling to his next station. No such luck. An hour after graduation, he was taken to the airport to wait for his flight to Virginia.

He called from the airport that evening. Nonchalantly he shared, "By the way, I almost got shot when we were doing some night exercises with live fire. Someone told our squad leader 'shift left' and didn't tell the squad leader for the other team to hold their fire. Then I saw a tracer bullet whiz past my knee. Our sergeant was mad!"

I tried not to think about the injuries and accidental deaths that occasionally occur during infantry training.

That same night I wrote:

> I'm struggling to keep my anxiety at bay. I was dreading yesterday [Halloween] because of the threat of terrorist activity. I'm trying hard to remind myself that new terrorist attacks are not happening yet—and they may never... Now the Golden Gate, Bay Bridge, etc. are supposedly threatened. It's only a matter of time till the West Coast gets hit. It's frightening to think how much havoc can be raised with our economy if the bridges are destroyed. Even the threat makes us spend so much money to deal with it. How can our economy cope? This is all so scary. It's easy to feel hopeless and defeated. But I'm trying not to.
>
> I feel as if I'm barely held together. And I'm very anxious about Daniel. I know I don't need to worry about him yet. But my heart is so heavy; I feel as if I have a hole in my heart. It's always barely beneath my consciousness.

We all were nervous in those early days, but my specific worry for my son played against the backdrop of my chronic anxiety.

I tried to tell myself that God would take care of Daniel. Intellectually I believed that. But believing it did not bring me any solace. Bad things also happen to people who believe God will take care of them. Rather than beg God to do my will, I decided to pray for God to be with Daniel, that

Daniel would know he was by his side, no matter what happened. I wish I could say that I came to a peaceful acceptance of whatever was in God's plan for me, but I could not sustain any acquiescence beyond a few minutes. Almost immediately I would find myself begging God not to ask me to give up my son. I withered before the image of Abraham wanting so fervently to obey God that he would sacrifice his son. I doubted I would have been that obedient. The entire four years I went round and round with myself about this. I suspect this is a difficult issue for many others whose loved ones serve.

Chapter Eight

SECURITY FORCE SCHOOL

In accordance with his contract for a Security Force MOS, Daniel arrived on the first of November at Chesapeake, Virginia, for training. Once there, he was told the next set of classes at Security Force School would not start till January 2 and that he would probably spend the two-month interval doing menial grounds-keeping chores on the base. He found the idea of doing mindless things for two months very irritating. Then, close on the heels of this announcement, the timetable changed. The start date shifted from January 2 to November 5.

The change in Daniel's class schedule was the first of many signals that the military mind sometimes defies logical interpretation.

There is a tongue-in-cheek expression that plays on the Marine's motto "Semper Fi" (a shortened version of "Semper Fidelis," a Latin phrase meaning "Always Faithful"): "Semper Gumby." This is an indirect reference to the unusually limber animated figure, Gumby, and jocularly refers to the attitude of flexibility we families need to maintain vis-à-vis the Marine Corps.

It sounds ludicrous now when I say this, but for the first three years Daniel was in the Marine Corps, I honestly thought I would be able to figure out the thought processes of commanders. There had to be logic to the monolithic military mind. Only in Daniel's last year did I finally give up the futile effort.

Daniel called the first week he was in Virginia to tell us that Security Force School would observe the national holidays and that he had chosen Veteran's Day for his liberty, in lieu of Thanksgiving, in order that a married Marine with children might have family time at Thanksgiving instead. The Marines had already been told it was unlikely they would be home for Christmas.

I bought Daniel a plane ticket on American Airlines so he could come home for the Veterans' Day holiday weekend, less than two weeks away.

I looked forward to getting my arms around Daniel. When speaking of her own Marine son, a member of our support group, Chris, stated, "After a while you start to miss the tactile sense of your child." That rang so true for me that I have never forgotten it. I had seen Daniel only a month before, but I already missed being able to touch him.

When he came home that Veterans' Day weekend, I sometimes reached out to pat his head. I especially loved to run my hand up the back of his shaved head; the bristly feel of his close-shaved head on my hand was so peculiarly ticklish. I tried not to do this very often because, understandably, he found it pretty annoying.

One of the things I did that weekend considerably improved my quality of life. I got Daniel a cell phone. Cell phones were not as omnipresent before 9/11 as they are now. I surmise one of the reasons that these have become so commonplace was the need people had, after September 11, to stay connected during an emergency as well as the realization that cell phones had provided several victims of 9/11 the means to say good-bye to their loved ones.

When Mario was in Vietnam, letters didn't reach the Marines for weeks, by which time any domestic crisis detailed in the letter would likely have been resolved. The remoteness of family issues left the Marine free to concentrate on his mission. When a Marine had a problem with his family or a girlfriend, only his buddies were available for support, and that encouraged intense bonding. Mario feels that today's instant communication with family hinders Marines from creating as strong a bond. Indeed, modern communication may interfere with a Marine's ability to fully adjust to being away from home. He might continue to be involved in family problems or, worse, still be expected to manage family issues long-distance. In Mario's opinion, as long as a Marine is actively involved with his family's day-to-day issues, he can neither be fully present to his family nor to his men in the field. I acknowledge Mario's point, and only time will tell if modern communication has been a hindrance or a boon.

Daniel protested that he didn't want a cell phone. I retorted that *I* needed him to have it. I found it so frustrating to never know when he would call, or to miss a call. For me, it was less important that he have the phone turned on. I was just relieved to be able to leave a message if I needed to, instead of waiting for two weeks for him to get around to calling me. This simple action of buying a cell phone purchased more than convenience for me; it purchased my peace of mind.

Eventually Daniel himself began to find the cell phone indispensable. Not only could he call home from the comfort of his barracks—instead of standing outside at a bank of pay phones in all types of weather—but, because he had unlimited weekend long-distance minutes available, he was also able to lend his phone to his Marine friends so they too could call home for free.

Since Daniel would not be home for Thanksgiving, we celebrated it while he was here for the Veterans' Day weekend. To my dismay, my daughter had to work, and the six of us were unable to celebrate it together. Trying to get the entire family together became a daunting task during the four years that Daniel served.

The evening before he left Chico to return to Virginia, some local active and former Marines celebrated the day the Marine Corps was formed, November 10, 1775. Every year Marines throughout the world celebrate the Marine Corps birthday—typically with a formal ball to which they wear their dress blue uniforms. Even Marines in a combat zone celebrate in some fashion. My husband is fond of repeating an old saw: "Every Marine has two birthdays—his own and the Marine Corps'."

For years a local Marine veteran has organized the annual birthday festivities for area active duty and veteran Marines. This year both Mario and Daniel were able to attend. Daniel's Marine recruiter and his wife were the guests of honor. While most guests wore business attire, both the recruiter and Daniel wore their dress blues.

The standard birthday ritual was followed: recitation of a letter written in 1921 by former commandant General John A. LeJeune as well as the birthday message from the current commandant of the Marine Corps. A cake decorated with the Eagle, Globe, and Anchor emblem is cut with a ceremonial sword. The oldest Marine present receives the first piece; the youngest gets the second piece. At age 18, Daniel was honored with the second piece of cake.

Tuesday, the day after the Veterans' Day holiday, we took Daniel to the Sacramento airport. Ten minutes after his plane lifted off, our car radio news program announced that an American Airlines flight had gone down in New York. It was a while before we knew whether this was accidental or another terrorist action. Daniel's flight was due to land in Texas where he would change planes for the last leg of the trip. I didn't know if all the planes would be grounded again. I was wondering how it was all going, but luckily I could use that handy-dandy cell phone once Daniel arrived in Texas. Fortunately, air travel continued per usual and the remainder of his trip proceeded without a glitch. For me, his owning a cell phone was such a relief; I could relax now that I had communicated with him.

By the time Daniel left to go back to Virginia, I noticed an interesting phenomenon. While I didn't want Daniel to go back, I definitely was ready for the commotion of Daniel's visit to be over and to get my house—and my life—back to normal. I wrote in my diary:

> I am calmer, thankfully. With Daniel's visit, something shifted. I was able to see him more realistically. Yes, he's a warrior with a dangerous job, but he's still a self-centered teenager. I had been reluctant to give up my pain at his absence for fear that would make him more distant, less present, in my life. But I am ready to get back to my own life. I probably will miss him soon enough, but I don't have such a hole in my heart as I have had.… I can see this is healthier. In the end I will have to let him move away. I can stay connected, but I need to stay grounded in my own life.

Shortly after Daniel returned to Virginia, I opened an e-mail account for him, at his request. This was new territory for me; I had always been terrified to use computers. I feared somehow making the computer crash and losing all data. But the need to communicate with Daniel as well as with the Military Family Support Group offered me a growth opportunity. I began to value the easy and quick communication of e-mails. I learned to surf the web to find out all kinds of information about the military in my eternal quest to figure out the Marine Corps.

Despite Mario's misgivings about the hazards of instant communication, all of us eventually became grateful for it. E-mail access ultimately became an important part of our communication during Daniel's deployments.

Graduation from Security Force School was a few days before Christmas. Though Daniel had been told he wouldn't be home for Christmas, I still held out hope. He was such a homebody that I wished he'd be able to at least spend his first Christmas as a Marine with us.

As it turns out, Daniel's group wasn't even told whether they would be granted leave until the day of graduation—December 20. I had been reluctant to wait until then to buy an airplane ticket, for fear that, if he did get leave, there would be no more seats available. I had taken a wild gamble, buying a ticket for him weeks before, and had arbitrarily chosen Saturday, December 22 as his travel date. Luckily for me, I guessed well, but the military's inscrutability made it difficult for the families as well as the men. Whatever made me think I could figure the military out? At least he was permitted nine days of leave, but I wondered whether the last-minute nature of the command's decision meant that some Marines could not get home before Christmas.

Daniel had an odd notion that it would be fun to make his Christmas visit a surprise for his dad. Daniel concocted an elaborate ruse, telling his dad that he was unable to come home. Meanwhile, Daniel roped me into being an accomplice in the surprise. Daniel arranged for me to pick him up at the airport the evening of his arrival. Not only did I dislike the deception about Daniel's visit, but also I disliked fabricating a lie to explain why I would be out late, by myself, on a Saturday night. Moreover, I thought it was mean to intentionally toy with his dad's emotions. Indeed, Mario was so sad that he wouldn't see Daniel for Christmas that several times he had nearly broken down in tears. I reluctantly kept my promise to Daniel, because I knew it would turn out well in just a few days.

Sadness was always under the surface. The night before Daniel's arrival, as I dusted picture frames, I started crying when I came to Daniel's boot camp graduation photo because I missed him—even though I knew I would see him the next day.

I still was nervous about the safety of flying post 9/11, and not without good reason, it turns out. The so-called "shoe bomber" tried to ignite an explosive during an international flight the very next day.

At 11:00 PM, when Daniel and I drove down our street, the block was still aglow with the neighborhood Christmas light displays. My role was to awaken Mario, telling him that I had gone Christmas shopping and needed him to get a large package out of the car—tonight. Mario is never one who wakens well. He grumbled that whatever was in the car could wait till the morning. At my insistence, he crossly got out of bed, making his way towards the living room. Daniel, who had been hidden around the corner, then popped into view. Mario's reaction, though muted by grogginess, was relief and joy. Nonetheless, I never want to conspire to play a trick like that again.

Lots of family came to spend the holidays with us. I was glad this could be a Christmas Daniel could remember fondly if indeed he wouldn't be home for the holidays next year.

Daniel's return flight was scheduled for New Year's Day. As the day approached, as with previous occasions, the heaviness in my heart increased. In many ways it was just better for him to go and get it over with. There was so much more poignancy in his leave-taking than if he was a student returning to college; I was always mindful of the seriousness of his job.

During that winter, I continued to wrestle with my conflicting emotions about war and the appropriate government response to terrorism:

> I am surprised at how differently I view our actions in Afghanistan from my usual view on war. I really do think fighting seldom accomplishes anything, and war is uncivilized. But then Al Quaeda was not looking for compromise or negotiation. Their intent is to destroy us! Yes,

I mind that we're killing so many people with our bombing—especially the innocents. And I think it is appropriate to try to target specifically to minimize "collateral" damage. But it seems as if, once at war, it's a different ball game.... Now that we have been put in a position of saving ourselves because of an unprovoked attack, offensive action ought to be appropriate and moral. But is it? If killing is all so uncivilized, how can it be okay—even sometimes? But what other choices would have worked? What if they nuke a city or spread biological warfare? Will I feel the same? And yet I feel—ugly as that scenario is—we may need to adjust to the notion biological warfare and other acts of terrorism against Americans could happen and the deaths from that would be *our* collateral damage, a price we may have to pay to win a war we can't afford to lose.

Chapter Nine

1st FAST 2002

Upon his return to Virginia in early January, Daniel was given his assignment for the next two years. He would be stationed at the naval base in Norfolk, Virginia. He was to be a member of a specialty force: Fleet Anti-Terrorism Security Team (otherwise known as FAST).

The FAST companies were established in 1987 under the umbrella of the Marine Corps Security Force Battalion. (Not to be confused with the Marine Security Guard Battalion, which provides security to American embassies and consulates).

Though the number is higher now, at the time Daniel served, there were more than 500 Marines in Fleet Anti-Terrorism Teams. Twelve platoons were distributed into two companies. Daniel's company, 1st FAST, consisted of seven platoons. The other company, 2nd FAST, which had five platoons, was located nearby in Yorktown, Virginia. (3rd FAST, also headquartered in Yorktown, wasn't formed until after 2001).

The main purpose of FAST companies is defensive: to protect vital Navy and national assets and, according to a 2006 Marine Corps Web site description of FAST, "for a limited duration." Traditionally FAST members do not perform counter-terrorist activity, and rarely have offensive missions. Approximately a dozen Marines from each platoon are trained in close-quarters combat. In essence, FAST is a rapid-response unit that can go anywhere in the world on short notice. The responsibilities of F.A.S.T are as varied as base guard duty during situations of heightened terrorist threat, hostage rescue, and urban combat. The function of the team while Daniel was a member was to arrive anywhere in the world within a few days, secure an area, but not remain for long-term activity. The focus in those days was to be the security force for the Navy. The Chief of Naval Operations, the Marine Commandant, or the Commander-in-Chief could call FAST teams into action.

Though Marines like to think of themselves as a separate branch of the military, they really are a part of the Department of the Navy. Hence, the role of FAST to protect the Navy's vital installations around the globe, as well as its ships. For example, FAST members were sent to secure the Yemeni port of Aden following the attack on the *U.S.S. Cole* in September 2000.

When Daniel arrived at his new assignment, he joined other Marines being trained for the 4th Platoon, 1st FAST. To be ready for deployment, the newly-arrived Marines needed five more weeks of training including advanced biological and chemical warfare response (which meant more "gas chamber" training, but with a more noxious substance than that used in boot camp), enhanced marksmanship and training in Squad Automatic Weapons (SAW), urban assault, and hand-to-hand combat.

I reassured myself with the knowledge that Daniel was getting extensive training with elite weapons and gear. Even if he would be sent to a combat region, historically, FAST missions had been short-term. (FAST companies' operational policy was soon to be altered. Teams were deployed in the opening phase of Operation Iraqi Freedom in 2003 and in 2004 for a yearlong tour in Afghanistan to secure our embassy.)

February 2, 2002, was Daniel's nineteenth birthday. I threw my energy into putting together what I called a "party in a box" for him. Daniel begged me not to send him any gifts; he didn't have space in his cramped room for any more possessions. The only space available for clothes and personal belongings was a small closet and footlocker.

Ignoring him, I bought some goofy kids' toys: a spongy football and basketball, a deck of cards, toy racing cars, and bubbles. I baked a carrot cake, froze it, and then placed a cake and toys in a box along with our family's traditional homemade "Happy Day Cake," plastic utensils, cups, powdered Kool-Aid, candles, matches, and party hats. I thought maybe he and his buddies might have fun tossing the soft football around in the barracks. If they themselves didn't use the toys, they could give them to the Marines with children. He seemed somewhat mystified or maybe embarrassed by the nature of the gifts. I suspect I was more disturbed by not being with Daniel on his birthday than he was.

Daniel had told me that he and his buddies liked to spend most of their free time going to the mall. I called the business office of the mall in Norfolk to buy a gift certificate for his birthday. I mentioned to the mall manager that it was Daniel's first birthday away from home. When the certificate arrived in the mail, there was a note attached to it that touches me still:

> Dear Nanette, It must be rough with Daniel away for his 19th birthday. We all do certainly appreciate the young men serving our country, especially in these most unsettling times. You are brave and I know he is too. I hope your gift brings him some smiles. Debbie

Throughout Daniel's service there were occasions like these when strangers reached out to me to say "thank you," offered to keep Daniel in their prayers, or honked and gave a "thumbs up" in acknowledgment of the Marine stickers on my van. What morale boosters those gestures were. Sometimes during those four years, I was feeling so raw that gestures like this made a difference in my day.

Daniel achieved the rank of Lance Corporal in March of 2002. About this same time he was able to come home on a ninety-six hour liberty in time for Easter. It was great to see him, but, as always, difficult when the time came to have to say goodbye yet again. He informed us that he had been chosen to take Close Quarters Battle training (which entails hand-to-hand combat) as soon as there was an opening in the next class. The week after his return to Virginia, he also expected to begin Bounty Hunting School, which was being offered to FAST Company members. My mind groaned at the notion that such training meant he was being prepared for more perilous circumstances.

I tried not to spend too much time worrying about it, but I wasn't often very successful. I was reminded of a silly fairy tale I read in grammar school about a woodsman's wife who one day began to cry when she noticed that her husband's axe was mounted on the wall. Her husband came by and asked her why she was crying. She sobbed that she was thinking that someday they might have a son who might happen to stand underneath the axe as it accidentally fell from the wall. Their son could be killed. In the fairy tale, the husband then started sobbing, as did a neighbor who came along, until another villager suggested they merely place the axe elsewhere. Unfortunately, though I could see the folly in my worrying so much, I had trouble disarming it.

I should have remembered my friend Semper Gumby. While the entire platoon took the Close Quarters Battle Training, Daniel never did go to Bounty Hunting School.

The anxiety that both Mario and I felt about Daniel in the early years was probably not as much about Daniel as it was about our own previous experiences. We both were worried that the young men in today's military might be spurned, as the Vietnam vets had been. The emotional climate of 2002 was such that it seemed unlikely that would happen. I worried for Daniel as if he were going to war any second. For Mario, it was almost as if *he* was a young Marine again and about to go to war.

In April, the 4th Platoon was called to Bremerton, Washington, the location of a major Navy base to maintain security while an engine for a nuclear-powered ship was repaired. Because of its nuclear components, the engine was considered to be a possible target for terrorists or radical activists. For several nights after their arrival, Daniel's platoon was awakened repeatedly to practice securing the nuclear site within minutes. They practiced until their timing was sleek.

The assignment in Washington was supposed to last approximately two weeks, but lasted three months. For us it was a boon since Daniel was on the same coast, and we were able to see him three times in the three months before he returned to Norfolk in early July.

In late July, Mario, Clarissa, and I flew out to Norfolk to see him as we had previously planned to do. Our oldest son Mario planned to drive Daniel's car to Virginia a few weeks after our visit, so Daniel could have his car while stationed in Norfolk. Our middle son was working all summer as a camp counselor and was unable to accompany us.

The day we arrived in Norfolk, while we waited for Daniel to get off duty, we took a base tour, given by Navy personnel. Norfolk is host to the largest naval base in the world. The base proper covers an area of 4,631 acres and is home to almost eighty ships (not all in port at the same time). It employs 11,000 civilian workers and about 8,000 military workers. Our tour guide told an impressive story relating to a time just prior to Daniel's assignment to FAST. On September 11, 2001, the order was given for the Marines to secure Norfolk Naval Base within five minutes. The 350 or so Marines of 1st FAST fanned out to all parts of the base and closed off all entry gates to the base. No one was permitted to leave or enter the base. The Marines secured every one of the base's twenty-two gates that day in an amazing three and a half minutes.

One of the places Daniel especially wanted us to visit was that icon of popular culture—the local Hooters restaurant, the other favorite place where Daniel's off-duty Marine friends liked to hang out. Sure enough, when we arrived, there was a table of other FAST Marines.

It was reassuring to be able to visualize the places in Daniel's world; my anxiety level dropped considerably after the visit. It was, all in all, a really delightful trip.

My husband's Marine Vietnam veterans' group had a reunion, which coincided with the Marine Corps birthday and Veterans' Day, in November in Washington DC. On this occasion, Daniel drove from Norfolk and joined Mario and the other veterans for the weekend activities. Daniel had a hundred fathers that weekend. I later asked, "Did you mind everyone giving you advice?"

"No, not really. I don't mind taking advice from people who have seen combat. At least they know what they're talking about. They told me to keep low and, if I'm ever in a jam, follow my instinct."

Personally, I thought that last suggestion—to listen to intuition—very apt.

Mario was very proud of Daniel and pleased to be able to introduce him to his Marine buddies. One comment of Daniel's gratified Mario very much. "Dad, I know you always talked about the brotherhood of the Marine Corps. Now, watching these guys with each other and how they are with me, I understand for the first time what being a Marine means."

The year 2002 was idyllic for us. The world was relatively calm, and Daniel had not ended up in harm's way. And, improbably, that year, at least some member of our family got to see Daniel nearly every two months.

Nonetheless, by fall, there were obvious clues that the country was preparing for war. Not only was there talk of weapons of mass destruction that were believed to be in Iraq, but some parents in our support group reported their sons were being told they might be going "somewhere" soon, and needed to get their affairs in order.

It seemed likely that Sadaam Hussein did have weapons of mass destruction. I certainly believed his actions to be evil, and the world would be better off without him in power. Nonetheless, I wanted the government to outline a legally and morally tight rationale for war. Was it morally justifiable to strike the first blow? Conversely, if there are weapons of mass destruction, is it immoral *not* to take pre-emptive action, when such action perhaps might save thousands? Would it have been more moral in World War II to try to stop Hitler long before he began his panzer movement across Poland in 1939? These point/counterpoint issues sparred in my mind, and still do.

I wanted any action to be done properly. I wanted those in power to weigh the issues carefully and not place the military in a position of doing something that might later be construed to be morally unjustifiable. Though I realized the public might not be privy to all the facts surrounding the decision to go to war, I wanted to trust that any call to war would be a thoughtful and well-considered one, that the morality of the options had been considered. Since the President was my son's Commander-in-Chief, I decided to voice my concerns in a letter to him. I sent copies to President Bush, Vice-President Cheney, Secretary of Defense Rumsfeld, Secretary of State Powell, my two senators, Barbara Boxer and Diane Feinstein, and my representative, Wally Herger.

September 2, 2002

Dear Mr. President,

I have never written a political letter before, but I have such a level of concern regarding our stance toward Iraq that I feel impelled to do so.

I am concerned that the United States appears to be contemplating making a "first strike" attack on Iraq based on the presumption that Iraq is manufacturing weapons of terror and mass destruction. While perhaps it might be justifiable to attack first if there were incontrovertible proof of manufacture or storage of such weapons, it does not seem moral to be the aggressor based on assumption rather than proof. To me, taking the initiative against a sovereign country is of grave moral concern. It is an act of a bully. We would not countenance similar activity from another country. If we have such *proof*, or if Iraq refuses a new request for an unfettered weapons inspection by the United Nations in a reasonably defined amount of time, then one can begin to build the moral case. I would like to see an algorithmic approach to our policy that can set the tone to morally justify any offensive action.

I have a son who is currently serving in the Marine Corps. If he is put in harm's way or—God forbid—should have to pay the ultimate price in Iraq, I would be proud of his service to his country. But please don't let him die in a war that is not morally justified.

An additional concern is that if we act without setting the parameters that could morally justify action, we risk losing our allies' support. Acting alone is likely to result in a higher casualty rate. Once our military casualty rate or the civilian casualty rate gets high, we risk loss of support of Americans here at home if we are perceived to be the aggressor. I have a husband who was a Marine combat veteran in Vietnam; I am very sensitive to the issue of our military fighting in a war that is unpopular at home. I don't want my son to come home and be spat upon or called "baby killer" for doing the job his country asked of him. I can't bear the thought of enduring that nor the country going through that rancorous quagmire again.

If action must be taken, please approach the issue slowly and methodically. Please build your case so that action is clearly of last resort and morally justifiable.

Respectfully,
Nanette Sagastume

Interestingly, my senators and representative sent an answering form letter within a few weeks. Much to my surprise, I never heard from the Vice-President's office or the offices of Secretaries Rumsfeld and Powell. In the end, I eventually heard from what I assume was the President's staff—seven months later:

April 28, 2003

Dear Ms. Sagastume:

Thank you for your letter about Operation Iraqi Freedom. In Iraq, we sought to remove a threat to our security and to free the Iraqi people from oppression. Sadaam Hussein's regime has ended and the people are regaining control of their own country and future. Pockets of resistance still remain. American and coalition forces are helping to restore civil order, and providing critical humanitarian aid to the Iraqi People. Iraqis are already meeting openly and freely to discuss the future of their country.

Coalition forces have made every effort to spare innocent civilians from harm and continue to do so. We respect the Iraqi people, its rich culture and religious faiths. We will continue to bring food, water, medicine, and other aid to

Iraq, and we will help build a government of, by, and for the Iraqi people.

Our war on terrorism continues. We look to our Nation's Armed Forces, with the support of our coalition partners, to help advance peace in a troubled world. By answering the call of duty, these brave men and women serve as examples of courage, dedication, and sacrifice. Laura and I join our military families and countless others in praying that all who serve return home safely and soon.

Thank you again for writing. Best wishes.

Sincerely,
George W. Bush

After I wrote my elected leaders, I deemed that I had exercised my civic duty by voicing my concerns. I am not a protestor and, especially, I am not a demonstrator. I didn't expect that my letter would change anything, but it was important to me that I communicate my concerns. I feel blessed to live in a country where I am able to do that.

By the time the holiday season arrived, we again were able to have Daniel home for Christmas. Once again, I foolishly bought an airline ticket for Daniel in late October while airfare was cheaper and seats plentiful. A travel date set for a few days prior to Christmas seemed a reasonable gamble.

Semper Gumby! Between November and Christmas, Daniel's leave dates changed three times. Each reservation change incurred a hundred dollar penalty. Because Daniel wasn't traveling with orders, the airlines would not waive the penalty fees, even though the changes were not due to our whimsy, but to the Marine Corps'. By the time Daniel actually traveled, my "cheap" ticket had become almost twice its original price.

That Christmas our middle son, Damián, was not with us. He had become engaged earlier in the year and was traveling to Michigan to meet his fiancée's family. We once more confronted the continuing challenge—getting the six of us together at the same time. Daniel's Christmas visit was to be the last visit home before his deployment for six months to Yokosuka, Japan. Because Daniel's platoon was to deploy in the early days of January, Daniel was confident that he would be back in time to be best man at Damián's wedding, scheduled for July 19, 2003. Oh, how could we forget Semper Gumby?

Chapter Ten

1ST FAST 2003

FAST Company maintains platoons forward-deployed to several strategically located countries, in order to be more responsive to events around the globe. At that time, continuous six-month deployment rotations were organized in such a way that a platoon from 1st FAST relieved a platoon from 2nd FAST and vice-versa in each of these countries.

Unfortunately, the platoon from 2nd FAST, which Daniel's team was replacing in Japan, was delayed returning to Norfolk. This meant that Daniel's departure for Japan was now delayed till the last days of January 2003. The change in schedule meant that the chance of Daniel being back in time for Damián's wedding was extremely "iffy."

By January, the military was positioning itself for war. One of the women in our support group told us that her son's Marine unit was due to leave for Iraq in mid-January by Navy ship.

Daniel mentioned that his platoon was being issued chemical warfare suits and masks—which had not been issued to the platoon they were to relieve. The thought of Daniel being subjected to a chemical attack utterly horrified me.

Mysteriously, Daniel told us his platoon would deploy to Japan, but then would most likely be sent "elsewhere" within a week of arrival. Marines were also told that if "things start to happen, we could be in the middle of it all."

The "where" and "what" of this cryptic statement were not specified. Daniel seemed excited by the dramatic tone of these words.

Military confrontation in Iraq seemed imminent. The world would be changed irrevocably once we embarked on a war. I was afraid not only for my son and for others in the military but, also, for all Americans. Once this major step was undertaken, would we have courage to endure if our opponents began to retaliate against us? And what about the ordinary Iraqi citizens and the innocents who would suffer? I was afraid for them too.

Daniel left for Japan on January 31—several weeks later than in the original timetable. He tried to phone us several times during the next two weeks from public phones in Japan (his cell phone did not have international capability), but we seemed to always be out. Each time we came home and heard his voice on our message machine, Mario and I wailed with frustration to have missed him once again. Daniel had been in Japan for three weeks before we finally got to speak to him.

In the late winter months, his platoon spent a lot of time in training. In photos, in which Mount Fuji looms in the background, he and his buddies wear menacing Ninja-type gear: camouflage uniforms, body armor, black ski masks pulled up to their noses, and helmets under which only their dark eyes were visible. They held automatic weapons. I wouldn't have recognized which Ninja Daniel was if it weren't for the fact that I knew he was the shortest one. It was unsettling to see my child looking so menacing.

Through the winter, the United States seemed headed toward a showdown with Sadaam Hussein. An American military presence was building just over the Iraqi border in Kuwait. The drumbeats of war were reaching a feverish tempo.

On Saturday, March 15, while our family feasted on an early St. Patrick's Day meal, Daniel called. He sounded subdued.

"I just called to say goodbye because tomorrow we're supposed to go somewhere on the boat and I don't exactly know where. I don't know when I'll be able to call you again."

I peppered Daniel with questions he was not in a position to answer—a very annoying tendency of mine.

"All I know is that we will be somewhere. Honestly, Mom, I really don't know much more except we were told we will be going on an assignment."

I thought surely this meant Daniel would be going to Iraq. We passed the phone around to each family member so that we could say goodbye. Not knowing what to say in such a moment, his siblings offered hackneyed pieces of advice such as "Stay low" and "Stay safe." Our meal, which I had just brought to the table when Daniel called, cooled as we ignored our guests, instead taking turns speaking with Daniel. I managed not to cry while I was speaking to him, but then started sniveling at the table and had to abandon my guests once again to regain my composure.

A few days after this phone call, with the license of empty-nest parenthood, Mario and I left for a previously planned getaway, part of a conscious strategy to schedule several small trips to nurture ourselves during Daniel's deployment. On this occasion, we took advantage of the University's spring break and scheduled a mid-week escape to a little Victorian bed-and-breakfast inn in Sacramento.

During that week the situation with Iraq was coming to a head. After months of diplomatic skirmishes, on March 17, President Bush gave Sadaam Hussein a deadline of forty-eight hours in which Hussein and his sons, Uday and Qusay, must leave Iraq. If they did not go, Americans were pledged to respond.

Mario and I were grim. We had misgivings about going away to have a good time. The days we had arranged to be gone overlapped President Bush's ultimatum. We hardly felt festive, but we decided to go anyway. At least it was a diversion. The alternative, I knew, would mean that we would sit at home, watching the television news, and becoming more depressed. With some misgivings, we set off.

In the end, we probably ought to have stayed home. We tried to have fun, shopping in some of the stores in the quaint Old Town section of Sacramento. We even looked for yellow ribbon with which to make a large bow that we would place on the tree in front of our home until Daniel came home. Mechanically we browsed in stores and nibbled at food in restaurants. We found that we had many silent moments, lost in our own morose thoughts. When we did talk, it was about the situation in Iraq, the chances for military success, or our fears for our nation and for Daniel. We waited with ominous dread.

We looked about us at other diners who were gaily chatting and laughing as if the future of the world wasn't being molded at this moment. None of the conversations we happened to overhear seemed to even include any mention of the situation in Iraq. It felt to us as if people were unconcerned about world events because they would not be directly affected. The war wasn't happening in their backyard, nor would their sons be in combat. What we perceived—probably erroneously—as lack of concern on others' part made us angry. I wanted to scream, "Don't you care we are about to go to war? Don't you care that the lives of our sons and daughters in uniform are in jeopardy at this moment?"

The following afternoon, when the Bush deadline had elapsed without evidence that any of the Husseins had left their country, we retreated to our room at the inn to watch the President address our nation. We listened solemnly as he stated he had ordered military action against Iraq, which had, in fact, already begun.

As he spoke, fear for our military sons and daughters ignited my stomach, as well as for Iraqi citizens. Often I am able to appreciate opposing points of view. Likewise, my nursing education has trained me to anticipate the multi-faceted impacts of critical events upon individuals. So it wasn't much of a stretch that I pictured little children in Baghdad huddled with their mothers, as they sheltered in basements during the deafening "shock and awe" bombing. I prayed for these imaginary mothers who, frightened themselves, ached to soothe and protect their terrified children, but who were powerless to stop the apocalyptic din. Whenever I hear the phrase "shock and awe," that image springs up in my mind as vividly as if I was one of those mothers.

Mario and I were utterly depressed by the end of the President's message and just wanted the safety and comfort of our own home. We told the proprietor of the bed-and-breakfast that we would be leaving earlier than we had planned. We explained why we wanted to go home, reassuring him that his establishment was not at fault. Since we were checking out at dinnertime, we tried to pay for that night but the proprietor declined to take any money, saying it was his gesture of thanks for the service of our son. We were so dispirited, but the kindness of this stranger truly touched us.

Once again, I tried to piece together comments that Daniel had made over the months and decided that his FAST Company might be working with the British Royal Marines, with whom they had trained the previous summer. The Royal Marines were already on scene. Trying to sleuth my way through Daniel's various pieces of non-information, I thought that he might be in Iraq and, perhaps even more specifically, in Basra, which was in the British area of responsibility. This was all speculation on my part, of course. Because we didn't hear from Daniel for a few weeks, my imagination went into overdrive. To this day Daniel is tight-lipped about his participation in the opening days of the war. It's possible he was not in Iraq at the time, But I believed him to be there. Ultimately, the only factual information he will give me about that deployment is that during part of the six months he was gone, he was in a number of Asian countries, some of which he says he is prohibited from naming. He is baffled why the secrecy, but the Marines were told that the information was classified. Wherever he was, apparently his mission directly supported the War on Terror. Other than being aware that he spent part of his time aboard large ships, I'm no more knowledgeable now, years later, about his whereabouts than I was then.

We had a brief e-mail on March 20 advising us that he wouldn't be able to write us for a while. He said it was not likely that he would be at his current destination "too long," which I noted, with hope, as being consistent with the nature of FAST.

During the first few days of the war it felt as if the entire nation was glued to the television, while embedded reporters filed stories from the battlefield. The nadir was on Sunday, March 24, when an Army convoy was ambushed near Nasiriyah, resulting in American soldiers being captured. This was almost more frightening to me than had the soldiers been killed. I couldn't bear to think of what despicable tortures would be inflicted upon them. The entire nation had a front row seat to these televised dramas as they unfolded. This was tremendously unnerving.

One well-known news personality, embedded with a Marine Air Wing unit, reported with breathy excitement that a helicopter from the squadron with which he had been flying had just gone down, resulting in fatalities. Hearing this live report on television, one of the mothers in our support group called me, frantic because her son had phoned her only a few days previously to say his helicopter had been one of three escorting this same celebrated reporter. Realizing there was a very real chance that her son had been on board the downed helicopter, the mother was distraught. I was unaware of the Marine's bereavement team procedure and couldn't help her. I called another Marine mom in the group (coincidentally whose son's job in Iraq also involved flying in helicopters). She happened to have the phone number for the Marine Casualty Hot Line.

When the frightened mother called the Hot Line, she explained her concern to the Marine who answered. He was kind enough to look on his roster to see if her son's name appeared on the casualty list and informed her it was not there. That Marine saved our friend hours of unnecessary heartache. However, the incident highlighted new issues arising from modern advances in telecommunication, in which uncensored "this-just-in" kind of reporting occurs. These issues were not possible in wars of decades ago. The kind of technology that makes such immediacy possible barely existed in the first Gulf War, only twelve years prior.

This is the negative aspect of instant communication: it allows the viewing audience to be a part of the events. Because of a reporter's careless comment, some mother might learn of her child's death even before the official notification. We, as a society, have yet to flesh out the ethics and etiquette— let alone the security—for the new frontier of telecommunications.

One mother I know was terribly traumatized by a cable television network's frequent replay of footage of her deceased son's recognizable silhouette—still at the wheel of his military vehicle where he'd been killed.

On the positive side, the policy of embedding reporters with military units has enabled viewers and online readers to get news, information, and photos rapidly, affording them a real sense of being on the war front. The viewer feels the urgency of unfolding events, much as the troops do. That certainly makes for compelling footage and is just what caused many of us to be unable to move away from the television for weeks. Unfortunately, the immediacy of such instant communication also increases the anxiety for most of us.

I can recall a segment—a breaking story—that aired early in the war. A photographer with one of the major television networks was filming, live, from his room on an upper level of one of the Baghdad hotels popular with Western media. It was past midnight in Iraq; shadowy figures of Marines below had fanned out among the palm trees in the courtyard of the hotel to look for an insurgent sniper reported to be on the hotel grounds. I watched, fascinated, as the Marines approached a clump of foliage where the sniper was thought to be hiding. It was as gripping as a suspense film—till I suddenly realized, Oh, my God! What am I doing? I don't want to be watching someone's last moments on earth as if it were entertainment. I fled the room.

It may seem difficult to remember the level of fear and anxiety that we, as a nation, had as the war unfolded before our eyes. We know now that there were no chemical or biological weapons launched at our troops, but at the time we thought it was possible, even likely. Our men and women in Iraq wore protective clothing and gas masks. The fear that weapons of mass destruction might be used against our sons and daughters was chilling. And depressing. It was nearly impossible to perform the quotidian tasks of my life during this time.

There was a little flurry of media attention for my family in those first few weeks of the war. I cannot remember how the local newspaper learned of my support group, but a reporter called me and asked to attend the meeting that was being held that same evening. The newspaper wanted to focus on the effect of the war on local people, and the edition the following morning contained highlights of concerns voiced by parents at the meeting.

That April meeting was our first since the war had started. On the day of the meeting, our moods were more upbeat: Private Jessica Lynch had been rescued that same day (as it turns out, one member's son had played a role in that rescue mission).

Due to heightened anxiety, there was a larger group than usual at the meeting—more than twenty people piled into my house. There were members whose children had not been deployed to a combat zone but, nonetheless, they wanted to lend valuable emotional support to those with sons in harm's way. Some parents whose sons were in the Army asked to be in our group, and that night our group grew to embrace other branches of service. This support group was a good place to be—particularly for a panicked parent.

Our loved ones were scattered throughout the forces entering Iraq and, by stitching together the accounts, we began to sense the "big picture." While no parent had a lot of information about their child or his job, it helped to hear a parent talk about their worry for their child. Or of an e-mail they had received from their son. Or one they had not received. For some, hearing that other parents hadn't heard from their sons for weeks either, was reassuring. While there wasn't anything any of us could do to take away the pain of these parents, they often found deep comfort in our being companions in their anguish.

I tried to stay in touch by e-mail every few days with members whose sons were in harm's way. I, the computer-phobe, began to spend at least two hours a day writing to members of our group, and also surfing the Web sites to find all kinds of information for myself as well as for other members. This information spanned from trying to determine the location of various units to the family resource mechanisms for the various branches of service. The military has a valuable service called One Source, which has a twenty-four hour hot line, for members of all branches of the military or their families to access emotional, relationship, or work-related counseling (see Resources).

The stress of deployment was not exclusive to parents. An article in the local university's student newspaper, *The Orion*, addressed coping with the effects of the war on students (using my oldest college-student son, Mario, as an example) and the symptoms of stress. He is quoted as saying, "It doesn't matter where I am, I am always thinking about it.... I sit down to write a paper, and I just stare at my computer. The motivation is gone."

The local newspaper, the *Chico Enterprise-Record,* also ran an article highlighting the difficulty for my son Mario, who supported his brother but was very opposed to the war. As an elected officer in the University's student government, Mario was instrumental in getting the student government to pass a resolution in opposition to the war, though he specifically amended it to include an avowal of support for the troops. He had even marched at a large war protest in Sacramento. I am appreciative that the reporter, Roger H. Aylworth, dealt sensitively with my son's conflicting emotions of opposing the war yet wanting to support his brother, all the while fearing for his safety.

> When the shooting started last week, Mario's conflict between supporting a brother he loves and standing against a war he sees as unjustified suddenly became much more than a theoretical debate.... Before Daniel went overseas, and long before the shooting war broke out, Mario told his younger brother that if the war happened he would be protesting it. "He [Daniel] said that he would fight for my right to do that. He feels he is fighting for my First Amendment rights, and all my rights." (*Chico Enterprise Record*, March 26, 2003)

Mario's actions were incomprehensible to my husband. Public demonstrations against the government's policy in a time of war seemed, at best, disloyal and, at worst, akin to treason. War protesters marching in the streets were reminiscent of the Vietnam War era. My husband harbored a visceral loathing for Jane Fonda's Vietnam Era anti-war actions, particularly those in which she seemed to be in collusion with North Vietnam. He believes that demonstrations in wartime against one's country give solace to the enemy.

My husband was hurt to think his own son would do something that could put his brother at risk. Not only did he regard this as family disloyalty, it seemed treasonous to him. Our weekly family dinners often became battlefields. One evening's dinner began in its customary disorder. When I called everyone to the table, they spilled into the dining room looking for chairs, reminding me of puppies vying for a teat. Once seated, there began a cacophony of multiple conversations as the plates were passed around.

"Dude, will you pass the salad?"

"Mom, while you're up, can you get me some steak sauce?"

"Hey, can we start eating already? Do we have to say grace first?"

"Mom, could you come out of the kitchen so we can say grace and start eating?"

"Grace? Mom only says that when there's company so she can look good. I'm not waiting for any grace; I'm eating."

For a while there was only the sound of eating. Then my husband fired the first salvo.

"Did you see those idiots on the corner downtown, holding their antiwar signs? That really pisses me off! How can they protest when we're at war?"

Son Mario retorted, "But, Dad, this war is illegal, and people *should* be protesting."

"It's fine to exercise your civil rights and demonstrate *before* the war starts but, once it is started, then every American should close ranks and present a united front."

"But if our government is behaving immorally, I have an obligation to protest, Dad! We shouldn't be in Iraq. Afghanistan made sense; Iraq does not! Iraq isn't a threat to us; they had nothing to do with 9/11. Why are we there? Oil? My brother shouldn't be risking his life for oil!"

"It has nothing to do with oil! How could you even think that?"

"Okay, Dad, ask yourself this: If Iraq's main export was broccoli, would we still have invaded?"

"Mario, I can't believe you'd say something so stupid!"

The decibel level at the table increased. Forks paused midway. My stomach fluttered. Here we go again. Another family gathering is going to end in contentiousness, barbed words, and injured feelings. I wondered why, for once, couldn't we enjoy being together, rather than having to bicker over politics?

The voices at the table had a throaty edge to them, like the sound of two growling dogs circling warily, assessing each other. By now the other two children were starting to weigh in with their differing points of view.

Anxious to avoid a worsening situation, I frantically made a "T" with my hands.

"Guys, that's enough. Knock it *off*! We don't need this at the dinner table. No politics!"

It was as if my words were on "mute."

"I think Sadaam Hussein would have always been trouble and we were right to invade Iraq," my husband avowed.

"We have no business being there! I love my brother and I support him and all the troops, but I can't support a president who takes us into a war for dubious reasons and in a part of the world that already hates us. We are just going to make more terrorists. I love my brother and I want to keep him safe. In fact, I am going to the anti-war demonstration in Sacramento."

"I might go too," Damián, interjected.

"Well, that's just great! I don't know how you think that will help Daniel," Clarissa said.

My husband's face was a deep red, the veins in his neck dilated and pulsing. I massaged my constricted jaw muscles and jiggled my feet nervously under the table.

"Come on guys. *Please*?" I entreated. It was useless.

"You might think you're helping Daniel, but you're hurting him. You can say all you want to your senator. Write the president! But once you're at war, you do not demonstrate publicly. That only serves to give aid and comfort to the enemy by dividing the American people. You are making it *more* dangerous for Daniel!

"Only a traitor marches in an anti-war march now. I can't believe you would do anything that could risk the safety of your brother!" he shouted.

"Dad, it's *because* I want to keep him safe that I am doing this."

"If you march in the demonstration, you are not my son!" he roared.

Oh God, there it was—words that could never be taken back.

From somewhere was the sharp, shocked intake of breath.

The day after this debacle I reminded Mario that his father sometimes said very hurtful things when he was angry, but that, regardless of what he said, he loved his children very much.

"Yeah, Mom, I know. Still, I can't believe Dad even said that to me," Mario said, shaking his head in disbelief.

Indeed, later on the night of the dinner, my husband rued his words. But he never apologized.

I now am at the point where I can't bear to have certain topics brought up for discussion for fear of the outcome. To this day, I am the watchdog at family gatherings, struggling to keep conversations away from political discussions—which inevitably deteriorate into verbal frays.

For a short time after the Iraq war started I kept Mario company in front of the television set, which was virtually locked onto his favorite cable news station during all our waking moments—so much so that the station's logo burned its shadow onto the television screen. However, I eventually disciplined myself to walk away from the television set in order to keep my anxiety level from catapulting to a paralyzing level. I devised a strategy of listening only to brief hourly news bites a few times each day. I went online to the *New York Times* Web site where I only read the headlines—enough to have cursory awareness of world events—and I read in depth only what I could tolerate. At first, I felt guilty for not being exhaustively informed. But, ultimately, it was really the best decision at that time for my peace of mind.

Going to work regularly, where things hummed on as if life was normal, helped to keep me from being overwhelmed. However, as a retiree, Mario had too much time on his hands. Without the necessity of leaving home every day for work, he found himself nailed to the couch, watching the news. He grew increasingly more depressed as he worried for his son and our troops. With his mood dipping, he felt increasingly useless and put on the shelf, a Marine "has-been," whose warrior wisdom was no longer needed or valued in today's military.

He began to refuse social invitations and to renege on invitations he had previously accepted. "I'm just not in a party mood" or "I can't party when my boy might be in danger" were his refrains. During this time I went to many social engagements without him, but I know that people were sometimes hurt by his behavior. A few understood that he was having a difficult time. Most were bewildered by his seeming lack of manners.

Mario's social world began to constrict to his being just with me or with those family members with whom he felt a political solidarity. For him, an individual's political stance could be a deal-breaker. He often retreated to his sailboat, where his soul was nurtured. There were moments when the darkness of Mario's mood palpably lingered over the couch where he spent most of his days.

My mood was also precarious; there were times when I found myself outrageously sentimental. I hummed the song *Somewhere Out There* (from *American Tail*) to comfort myself that Daniel was really out there somewhere and could see the same pale moon. It seems so maudlin as I write this, but, at the time, it did make me feel better.

It surprised me that, not having before paid much attention to Jesus' mother Mary, I now began to feel a connection with her. I had a greater appreciation for the anguish she must have felt watching her son suffer. I was comforted thinking that, as a mother, surely she would understand the pain and worry I felt for my son; I found myself talking to her when I was really troubled.

Two weeks into the war, my husband's brother had a heart attack while he and his wife were vacationing in Mexico. This emergency situation would be stressful enough by itself, but in this case the situation was aggravated by the fact that his brother's American wife was stranded in a foreign country without being fluent in its language. Mario flew to the Mexican resort to assist them for a week before they flew back to the United States.

While in Mexico, Mario noted the opposition of Mexico's local television station and newspapers to America's involvement in Iraq. He called me several times to rant about what he'd seen. "Spineless" and "short-sighted" were words he spewed about the country of Mexico. He took it personally that other countries, particularly those that look to the United States for help, would not support our country. Mexico became the first in a list that has grown over the years of nations the he feels have turned their backs on the United States and which he avows never to visit.

With the beginning of the Iraq War, Mario's previously-tamed anger roared to life. I could see that he had over-identified with the United States. To criticize our country was to reject him. He interpreted events through the prism of the Vietnam years. Anything that seemed to be reminiscent of the antipathy displayed to our military made him pugnacious. His increasing self-isolation, his depression and the anger that masked it, were clear signals to me that his post-combat stress had been reactivated by the Iraq War and that, in fact, his PTSD was very much alive and intrusive.

Mario's life revolved around the television news. My life revolved around my connections to the military parents in our support group—particularly those whose sons were on the ground and air as our troops moved on to Baghdad. Mario participated in the meetings and had some very helpful things to say, but I was the one who organized it, nurtured it, and ran the meetings. Some of us moms occasionally met on the weekends for a happy hour or a Moms' Night Out dinner. These things did help to keep our spirits uplifted. Fortunately for those in the support group, all our children came back uninjured that year.

On April 17—the evening before Mario's birthday and when his spirits were their lowest—Daniel called from Guam to say he was returning to Japan. In a nanosecond, Mario's mood soared from nadir to zenith. He proclaimed that phone call was the best birthday present he'd ever had.

Over the next several weeks Daniel traveled by ship to countries around the Pacific Rim before finally returning to his base in Japan. Leaves are not granted during deployments except for family deaths or life-threatening illness involving an immediate family member. Alas, though the mid-July wedding was only three weeks before his revised scheduled return to the U.S. mainland, Daniel was not permitted leave, and the wedding went on with an alternate best man. Not even for the occasion of a family wedding could we all manage to be together. Semper Gumby.

Daniel completed his deployment in the second week in August. On his way back to Norfolk, he called me from the Detroit airport to let me know he had entered the United States. As soon as I hung up the phone, I burst into grateful sobs. My reaction startled me. I hadn't realized, till that moment of relief, that having him so far away—even in the relative safety of Japan—had subtly gnawed at me.

Daniel took some leave shortly after the return to his base in Norfolk. While he was home, we gathered people from the Military Family Support Group and other friends to welcome him home.

Daniel and another Marine friend, also on leave, were given plaques by the City of Chico, acknowledging their service in the cause of the Global War on Terror. It was a wonderful gesture for the city to make.

For the first time in a long time, all six of us—seven now with Katie, Damián's new bride—were able to be together before his week of leave dissolved. Until Daniel's enlistment, going to the airport had been fun; it meant greeting a loved one or going on vacation. However, rather than becoming easier, saying goodbye was still very painful. Even now, I experience a residual sadness whenever I go to the airport.

By the fall, Daniel's two-year tour in the Fleet Antiterrorism Security Team was winding down. The entire 4th Platoon's term was to end by December, with only a few staying on for another tour. The remaining platoon members received new assignments. Some were afraid they'd miss out on the action in Iraq. Mario makes the analogy that, like an athlete who has spent years training for the Olympics, a Marine wants the opportunity to finally put his training to the test. Daniel's MOS was infantry. Now that his commitment to FAST was drawing to a close, he "owed" the Marine Corps the remainder of his enlistment in a traditional infantry position.

Daniel began to seek ways to be reassigned to the same infantry unit his father had served with, the Second Battalion, First Marine Regiment of the First Marine Division (known familiarly as 2/1). More specifically, he wanted to get assigned to the same company, Fox Company, and eventually the same platoon, the 3rd Platoon.

At first, I was amused that Daniel was once more following in his dad's footsteps. After all, the battalion had already deployed to Iraq during the invasion and was now stateside. Other units hadn't even been to Iraq yet; surely those would deploy instead. If Daniel were to be assigned to 2/1, it was reassuring to think he wouldn't deploy to Iraq.

Oh, Semper Gumby. Be careful what you ask for; you may get it. On November 2, Daniel called to say he'd been assigned to 2/1 (the good news), but (the bad news) the unit would again deploy to "the Middle East," probably in April of 2004.

The role of the Marine Corps has traditionally been "the tip of the spear," moving offensively on land for the purpose of capturing territory. Formed as an expeditionary, amphibious force of the Department of the Navy, the original intention was that Marines would not be very far from their shore-base or the supplies aboard the ships that brought them to the land combat theater. The Marine Corps has always been a force that goes into an area with its infantry, subdues a territory, and then withdraws, deferring the peacekeeping and rebuilding of infrastructure to the Army. Of course, during the Vietnam War, the distinctions blurred somewhat, but generally speaking, that was the operational policy.

Several days before Daniel's phone call to us, a change in policy at the Department of Defense altered the mission of the Marine Corps. Secretary of Defense Donald Rumsfeld had announced that, in the face of the growing insurgency, Marines would be returning to Iraq to help with the gentler task of keeping peace. It was rumored that the Department of Defense wanted Marines to have longer deployments than their standard six to seven months, but that the Commandant of the Marine Corps "went to the mat" to keep the existing training schedules, arguing that longer deployments would significantly and adversely affect existing training schedules throughout the Corps. In the end, the Marine Corps retained the six-month deployments. However, instead of two six-month deployments per four-year enlistment, Marines could expect at least three deployments of six to seven months in a four-year enlistment.

It was said by many that the change in mission style and frequency put a strain on the Marine Corps to adapt as quickly as necessity dictated.

With the news of Daniel's impending deployment to Iraq, I tried not to slip into what I named "prophylactic grief." After all, April was a long way away. I tried to concentrate on Daniel's long leave in December as he relocated from the East Coast to the West. My husband made plans to fly to Norfolk in early December and to help Daniel drive his car and belongings home. I played long-distance navigator as I used my computer to guide them around a major snowstorm that was building as they started to drive cross-country.

Between the extra leave Daniel was given to move to his new duty station and the leave he had accrued, he was home for nearly four weeks.

At Christmas, my husband's family and ours typically rotate hosting the extended family. Christmas 2003 was our turn. I made an effort to ensure that all the traditional customs and rituals were performed. I wanted to make sure this was a Christmas Daniel would remember fondly, just in case this was his last Christmas—a fear I could only whisper to myself.

I learned quickly that if I did try to speak to friends of my darkest fears, they couldn't tolerate it. They would quickly urge me, "Don't be so negative," and follow up by reassuring me with comments like, "Now you *know* nothing is going to happen to him!"

On one occasion I was sufficiently weary of being shushed up in this way, I snarled back, "No, I *don't* know that nothing will happen to Daniel—and neither do *you*!" I know these people meant well, but walling off my fears with silence only made them more potent. I craved the comfort of someone validating my fear rather than trying to argue me out of it. I knew, however, that people's responses were also due to their own unease with the possibility of Daniel's mortality.

In our support group, we knew our fears were well founded. It was enough that there were others in similar situations and who would be beside me as I went through this.

In fairness to those who were more dismissive of my fears, I must say—with no small amount of shame—that I was equally insensitive during the previous Gulf War. In 1990 Mario and I took a business trip to Boston with several couples from my husband's work. One lady's Marine son was in a staging area in Saudi Arabia during the military buildup prior to the Gulf War. I remember this mother expressed worry for her young son, and she worried that she might miss a phone call from him while she was on the trip. As she worried aloud, I thought with some annoyance, "What is her problem? Her kid will be fine! Nothing will happen to him! She's being way too overprotective."

My God, I can't believe I actually had that thought. Since I know that an attitude behind one's thoughts can be perceptible to another person, I can only hope this mother never guessed my thoughts. I hope someday to run into her again. I want to apologize profusely and say, "I truly get it now. I am so sorry."

I didn't volunteer my morbid ruminations about Daniel's deployment to Mario, though I would have felt better sharing them with him. I knew that he was struggling to keep his own composure. If he had indicated that he wanted to talk about his concerns, I would have gladly discussed them. But I saw that not verbalizing fears was his way of coping. Likewise, sharing my concerns with Daniel was out of the question. Everyone's equanimity was in delicate balance.

We had an enjoyable Christmas, but, once again, we were unable to all be together. Son Mario had, long before, made arrangements to travel to Europe to visit a girlfriend who was spending the year studying abroad. Damián could only spend twenty-four hours with us because he had purchased airplane tickets months before to spend the Christmas break with his wife's family. We tried to keep our Christmas celebration light-hearted and traditional. I was aware of Daniel's efforts to commit to memory scenes of togetherness with both his nuclear and extended families. When I asked about it, he said he wanted a repertoire of memories to draw upon when he was homesick in Iraq.

All too soon he had to check in to Camp Pendleton, just after the New Year, to begin his assignment with 2nd Battalion, 1st Marines for a deployment that would become the third of my four life-changing events.

Mario, on a hill north of Da Nang, Vietnam, when he served in a security platoon, 1967.

Mario, serving in a security platoon north of Da Nang, with his M-14. 1967.

Mario in Vietnam.

Mario, serving in 2nd Battalion, 1st Marines, leaving the perimeter at night. 1967.

Mario, serving in 2nd Battalion, 1st Marines, on a major operation, 1967.

Nanette and Mario Sagastume, September 30, 1972.

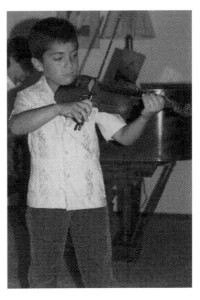

Daniel, age 5, frequently borrowed his father's utilities so he could pretend to be a Marine too.

Daniel, age 7, was a skillful violinist for the five years he took lessons.

All six of us: Front Row (left to right): Daniel, Nanette, Clarissa. Back Row (left to right): Mario (son), Mario (father), and Damián, 1999.

Nanette and PFC. Daniel A. Sagastume, November 10, 2001.

Daniel in his dress blue uniform, November 10, 2001.

Daniel, at sea, returning with 1st Fleet Anti-Terrorism Security Team from a mission in support of Operation Iraqi Freedom, Spring 2003.

Daniel, gunner for a convoy, in the turret of a Humvee, Fallujah, Iraq, 2004.

Daniel near Fallujah.

Daniel shaving, using the only mirror available—on his vehicle.

Daniel in Tower 77, just outside Fallujah, Iraq.

Battlefield Crosses for the Fallen at the base memorial service in Fallujah honoring the seven Marines and three Iraqi Special Forces soldiers, killed on September 6, 2004.

Nanette and Mario, December 2009.

Daniel with his bride, Violeta, December 2010.

Our grandchildren, Thanksgiving 2011.

Chapter Eleven

2ND BATTALION 1ST MARINES
PRE-DEPLOYMENT

In January we learned that Daniel's unit would be stationed in Fallujah, Iraq. My heart slumped. For the past six months I had been following news reports about Fallujah and knew it was deemed the most dangerous city in Iraq. The city seethed with insurgent activity. With good cause, I was terrified.

I found myself annoyed with people who, when I mentioned that Daniel was being posted to Fallujah, asked, "I never heard of it; which country is that?" I inferred that the questioners' lives were so insulated from the experiences of our military sons and daughters or even world news, that events in Iraq caused not even a ripple in their stream of consciousness. I was grateful for the people who said, "Oh no! Not there!"

From the moment I learned of Daniel's deployment, my emotional and spiritual turmoil intensified, and my trust in God was challenged. I whipsawed between begging God to spare my son and accepting my life, as I am given it. One moment I was willing to accept whatever God chose for my life; the next moment I would wail, "Please don't let him die!" When I did, with effort, surrender my will, I would be plagued by the fear that, by acquiescing, I might actually attract what I didn't want.

My mind became knotted in the age-old theoretical battle: Did God really will someone to die? Or, rather, does he share our sadness when he sees what we humans do to each other?

I was comforted that, on the night before he died, Jesus prayed to his father to let the cup pass. Even Jesus couldn't help having human reluctance to face the pain of suffering and death. Any solace that realization gave me, however, was short-lived. My next emotion was shame—shame that I should expect to be so privileged that I could avoid life's sorrows. Undoubtedly, other mothers whose sons had died must have prayed just as earnestly as I did.

I wish I could say that my spirituality was so deep and my trust in God so enormous that I left Daniel in God's hands and experienced an abiding peace. But that did not happen. The best I could muster was that I *wanted* to want God's will. I hung onto an image that the Lord had his arm around Daniel and our family, whether I felt his divine presence or not.

Perhaps one could say my faith wasn't great enough if I had that much fear. Perhaps that is true. Or, perhaps, my wrestling with God wasn't much different than Jacob's wrestling with the angel. I can only say that it was what it was.

Kristin Henderson, author of *While They are at War: The True Story of American Families on the Homefront*, speaks of a phenomenon, also discussed in the body of hospice and grief literature, called anticipatory grief:

> While my husband, a Navy chaplain, was in Iraq with the Marines, I imagined a knock at my door. I imagined uniformed Marines telling me that my husband was dead. I imagined the funeral. I did this regularly until my husband was safely home in my arms. I thought I was the only one with such a morbid imagination [I learned from the chaplains]…that when your spouse is in a combat zone, many of us have the same emotional reaction as someone whose loved one is dying from a terminal illness. It's called anticipatory grief, and the physical symptoms include everything from shortness of breath, like an anxiety attack,

to restlessness and agitation and difficulty concentrating. Emotionally, you're prone to crying jags. You find yourself imagining the funeral…. Not only had I not known all that craziness had a name—anticipatory grief—I had no idea other spouses were going through the same thing. (www.kristinhenderson.com).

I spent the entire four years of Daniel's military service in anticipatory grief. Certainly, my emotional meltdown when Daniel graduated from boot camp was anticipatory grief. From the time of Daniel's Fallujah assignment onward, I started to have moments when I visualized the Marine bereavement team at the door, the funeral and the people who might attend, or the songs we'd sing. I tried to picture myself as the grieving mother. Would I be calm or be wailing with consummate grief? And all this time these morose thoughts were a recognized coping mechanism. Who knew?

It was a relief to read that others went through this too. I thought it was something neurotically unique to me; in fact, I had given it my own name—"prophylactic grieving." I found myself trying on the worst possible scenarios as if, having practiced grief, maybe I could lessen its intensity, if the worst did happen. In retrospect, the logic falls short, lending itself to twice as much grief: once, in anticipation, and again, in reality. I had wasted precious time grieving for something that hadn't happened—time I could have spent instead enjoying the present moment. But emotions aren't logical.

Elizabeth, my spiritual mentor, suggested that, rather than be mired in anxious thoughts, I focus instead on the intention in my heart. She suggested that I ask God to watch over Daniel and then thank God for keeping Daniel safe for that day. I remember that I chuckled and said, "That will keep the negative thoughts away only for about five minutes, and then I'll be back to worrying."

Undaunted, she replied, "Then repeat that every five minutes if you need to." Indeed, I often needed to do exactly that throughout all the months of his deployment.

I realized I still needed to work at avoiding being emotionally entangled in Daniel's life. Until he became a Marine, I had never felt myself to be enmeshed in his life. But when he was in danger, my maternal instinct was in full throttle. I told myself I had my own life to lead. I reminded myself I could still care deeply without needing to over-identify with Daniel. Yet, subconsciously, I feared that by emotionally distancing myself from him, it was the equivalent of abandoning him somehow. Instead, I instinctively kept my emotional connection to him intense, as if the power of my desire that he live would ensure that he did. Surely, he couldn't die as long as I was so fervently willing him to live? As I write this, I know these were not reasonable feelings. Moreover, it was rather grandiose magical thinking. All I can say is that these subconscious feelings arose from some primal protective instinct; I was a tigress fighting for her cub's life.

To prepare for his deployment, I made a multi-dimensional personal plan of action (a nurse's care plan, if you will). My idea was to smooth my life as much as possible during this stressful time in order to enhance optimal coping.

I contacted the psychologist our family had seen from time to time over the previous decades, and scheduled monthly appointments.

After much brainstorming, I decided on some additional tactics to help me get through the difficult months ahead.

I already worked out regularly at the gym and ran most days of the week, so I would maintain those habits.

Since my sleep was interrupted many times a night by hot flashes, I decided to take female hormone replacement medication. Indeed, within a week of starting that therapy, instead of thirty or forty mini-awakenings, I began to sleep through most nights.

I also made sure I had access to quick-acting anti-anxiety medication—though I never remembered to take it when I could have used it. This supplemented an anti-depressant, which I had been on for several years. I have found that while I still experience appropriate sadness, the anti-depressant medication keeps my mood from falling off into an abyss. That was critically important now.

I typically received a massage once a month for chronic neck muscle tension, but I now made arrangements to receive massages every two weeks to keep my muscles loosened. I made sure I had soothing CDs at work to play during my breaks. And I continued to limit my exposure to the news—particularly television news. The visual image was too real and too frightening.

I also made a point to surround myself with things that lifted my heart. I surrounded myself with photos from nature, occasional nosegays of flowers, and calming potpourri. I made time for my favorite, soothing pastime—cross-stitching—though stress caused me to have difficulty concentrating on the craft.

And I made sure I maintained my daily habit of morning prayer time. I was powerless to control events, but I found it reassuring that I could at least pray for those people and events that concerned me. I sent all the love in my heart to Daniel. I had no doubt that my love would make its way to him—just the way mental energy from one person can be intercepted telepathically by another, even at a great distance.

Daniel reported in to Camp Pendleton shortly after the New Year. He had requested to be assigned to his dad's former unit. However, his superiors noted he was licensed to drive High-Mobility, Multi-purpose Wheeled Vehicles ("HMMWV," or more popularly known as Humvee). Much to his chagrin, he was told that, though he might be able to be reassigned to Fox at a later date, 2/1 needed experienced Humvee drivers and, for the time being, he would be assigned to H & S Company as a driver. Given all Daniel's specialized training in FAST, I was surprised those skills were not tapped.

Nonetheless, driving any vehicle in Iraq was dangerous due to the proliferation of Improvised Explosive Devices (IEDs) insurgents had planted alongside or in the road. Some have pressure plates that trigger an explosion when a heavy vehicle runs over it; some are triggered by remote control.

Over the weeks, not only did Daniel's departure date change, but also the mode of 2/1's transportation to Iraq. Originally Daniel's unit was to be part of a Marine Expeditionary Unit (MEU), which means the Marines would travel by Navy ship. The more time spent traveling by sea, the less time Daniel would be in Iraq. My relief at that good fortune was short-lived. Before long, the method of travel had changed to air transportation, with the departure date pushed up to early March. There it was again—Semper Gumby.

Indeed, there was a small upside to this; it would be a relief to get this over sooner.

For the next four or five weeks, the Marines trained for their mission. Training included house-to-house searches and hand-to-hand combat in a mock Arab city. Since 2/1 had deployed to Iraq the year before, some of this training reflected practical knowledge gained during the invasion of Iraq.

Knowing that Daniel would be with a combat-seasoned unit was reassuring. I was further cheered by the knowledge that he underwent excellent and extensive training in his FAST Company rotation. His Marine Corps skills had made Daniel as safe as it was possible for him to be, under the circumstances.

On January 22, 2004, Daniel called to say he had spent the day driving Humvees from Camp Pendleton to San Diego to be on-loaded aboard Navy ships. The heavy equipment and gear were being sent a month ahead of the troops.

Despite having known about this, the reality stunned me. It was actually going to happen. Improbably, I realized I had been hoping there would be some bureaucratic snag that would cancel the deployment. Where was Semper Gumby when *I* needed it? Moreover, now it turned out that Daniel would be deploying ahead of the rest of his unit, as part of the advance party. He was needed in Kuwait to help off-load the Humvees from the ships once they docked to be ready when the rest of the unit arrived. Daniel's departure date was February 28.

I was disturbed to know that the vehicles he loaded into the ships at San Diego were soft-sided. For weeks I was disquieted by that information. It was several months before I learned that, once the vehicles arrived in Kuwait, they were "up-armored"—armor plating was added to doors and/or to the floor of the vehicle and/or bulletproof windshields were installed. When Daniel arrived in Iraq he informed me that the vehicle he would be driving did have a bulletproof windshield. I decided not to torture myself further by asking about the sides of his vehicle.

I know that there was discussion whether our military had adequate personal protective armor. To the best of my knowledge, during that deployment, every Marine in 2/1 was equipped with Kevlar bullet-resistant helmets and inserts for their protective vests.

Daniel's uncle and his older brother Mario share the same birthday, February 3, and Daniel's is the day before. His uncle's wife wanted to have a party at her home for all three of them. This invitation was really very kind on their part, but it engendered a reaction in me that was petty, ungracious, and small-minded: I was jealous.

For Daniel, the party provided an opportunity for him to see his extended family before he deployed. He would be able to add to his family-memories treasury. The rational part of me realized that Mario's family had nothing but the best intentions. Yet, my mind whined, "But *I* wanted to give him a party for his twenty-first birthday. Maybe this is the last birthday he'll ever have, and *I* want to give the party!" I never gave voice to my thoughts because I knew Mario's family wasn't trying to compete with me.

Trying to make things easy, I was told that I didn't need to bring any food for the party. They already had a cake planned for all three Birthday Boys. Instead of being grateful, I minded that too. I knew that the party was for my brother-in-law, not only my sons Daniel and Mario, and my in-laws were the hosts. Nonetheless, I couldn't bear not having a role. Each year since I was ten years old I have baked a from-scratch "Happy Day" cake for family birthdays. After an inappropriate amount of time feeling sorry for myself, I asked Mario's family if I could bring my traditional cake to serve in addition to the one they planned. My sister-in-law good-naturedly agreed. I was ashamed then, and even now, at my childishness. Nonetheless, jealousy recurred from time to time. In fact, the entire time that Daniel was deployed, both Mario and I were surprised and dismayed at how very touchy, easily upset, and prone to self-pity we were.

On the birthday weekend, Daniel flew into the Bay Area. His aunt had arranged for a celebration that included a surprise visit by a trio playing mariachi music. We drove down from Chico for the event, and my husband's other brother even flew in from Colorado. Daniel seemed to have a good time, though at times tears glistened in his eyes as he watched family and friends conversing and dancing.

Not long after, on Valentine's Day weekend, he had a three-day liberty for the Presidents' Day holiday and he flew home. This was the last time he would visit us before deployment. Upon his return to base, his days would be spent in final training before he left with the advance party. He handed us some grim items—his Power-of-Attorney documents—in the event we might need to act in his behalf while he was gone (or, as all of us were afraid to mention, in case he died). Daniel stated that the Marines in 2/1 had been told to get their affairs in order and were ominously warned, "Not all of you will be coming back."

Daniel also brought Mario and me an extra set of dog tags. He told me that each Marine had been given six tags. Wondering if the Corps required so many tags in case the original tags were lost, I foolishly asked why the need to have so many sets. He answered that besides the tags around the neck, they needed to put one in each boot. I started to ask the reason for that, but the words died on my tongue as grisly comprehension trickled into my brain. My stomach lurched at the thought of my beautiful son losing a leg somewhere in the sands of Iraq.

For the entire deployment I rarely removed the dog tag. If I went to an event that was more formal, or if I wore an outfit that did not lend itself to dog tag accessorizing, I just tucked it into my bra, where it could still be close to my heart.

Though Daniel didn't want us to give him any items or gifts that would add to the hundred pound-plus pack he would be lugging, I gave him a small notebook in case he wanted to keep a journal, and I gave him a small pocket-sized New Testament as well. I thought he might find the words of scripture soothing when things were tough. I suspect both gifts were unused; they were really a reflection of what *I* thought he should want. I also gave him a gold cross on a sturdy chain, but he asked instead to take the more delicate cross and chain that Mario wore and which I had given him when we were married.

I gave Daniel a sealed envelope with a "love letter" from me for him to read when he might be downhearted. I am not sure he ever read it. His dad gave him a picture holy card—a small bookmark-sized card with an image of Jesus on one side and the Serenity Prayer on the other side. Mario's brother-in-law had given that very card to Mario before his deployment to Vietnam and he had tucked it inside the liner of his helmet for the thirteen months of his tour. He swore it had kept him safe in Vietnam; he was certain it would keep Daniel safe in Iraq too.

I packed Daniel's visit with various opportunities for us to get together. Damián and his wife came to Chico and, gratefully, we finally were all together.

Trying to keep the mood light, and to bundle the celebrations, I prepared a Valentine's Day dinner one night and an early St. Patrick's Day dinner the next—complete with all the decorations. Daniel had always enjoyed my corned beef and cabbage and Irish soda bread. Our attempts at jolliness were ersatz. Who can be merry while the Grim Reaper is standing in the corner of the room?

On the last night of his leave, the house slept in surreal stillness, I paced about the house, pausing at the doorway of Daniel's room, listening to his breathing. How could he sleep? How many times had I gone to his room to listen to him breathe when he was an infant? And how many times had I tiptoed in to stroke the smooth curve of his baby head or gently kissed the blanketed mound of his little behind?

All the trouble in his teens—years of his flirtation with gang culture, the lackluster academic effort, running away. Now he's finally got his life on track. So much effort on all our parts—would this be for nothing?

I ached to say, "Son, I have been blessed to have you for these twenty-one years. I love you so much. I am *so* scared I will lose you."

Afraid he would retort "Gee, Mom, cut it out!" I had forced the words back down my throat. I knew he would view such "last words" as melodramatic and might even worry they could jinx him. Besides, I knew I would be unable to utter them without weeping; the heaviness of suppressed feelings burdened me.

Drawn to my sewing room by its amber halo of lamplight, I rocked back and forth on my couch, struggling to stifle the keening that threatened to erupt from my throat. I was so sentimental that night that when I spied Daniel's stinky athletic shoe, I cradled it to my chest.

It was hard to concentrate on anything the next morning except the minutes crawling by until it would be time to take Daniel to the airport for his evening flight. I wandered about the house; reality was suspended, measured by the hours remaining. Six hours left. I tried not to stare as I focused throughout the day on Daniel's face, memorizing his features. The three moles across his left cheekbone. The bristles at the nape of his "high and tight" regulation haircut. The "tribal" tattoo on his lower leg. The way he smirked when he played a joke on me.

Five hours before he left. Four hours more to be with him....

It was Daniel who suggested, "Why don't we do something as a family? Why don't we go to the movies?"

That suggestion triggered a noisy debate. Our children couldn't agree which movie to see: one film was too silly for some; others objected that a different one was too violent.

Kristin Henderson mentions in *Ten Facts about Military Families that Civilians May Not Know* on her Web site (www.kristinhenderson.com): "Couples often pick fights just prior to deployment—subconsciously, it makes it easier to say goodbye." Were our children acting out a similar scenario? God forgive me, but I think we all just wanted the moment of goodbye to be over with.

In the end Daniel's suggestion won, and we saw *Miracle*, a film about the US Hockey Team winning the Gold Medal in the 1980 Olympics. Daniel's suggestion was actually a very wise way of distracting us, providing an entertaining—even inspirational—diversion and a chance for one final family memory.

All too soon it was time to make the ninety-mile trip to the airport. I stared out of the car window into the rainy and miserable darkness, tears coursing silently down my cheeks. Daniel played CDs in the car, filling the gaps of strained silence.

Once Daniel had checked in at the airline counter, we sat in the waiting area. The gloom pressed in on us. I didn't want Daniel to go, but I wanted the moment of goodbye to be over with. After shifting in our chairs for several moments, my husband suggested, "Daniel, this isn't going to be any better; we might as well go now."

We stood, each of us giving Daniel a bear hug. I was the last to take my turn. I squeezed him and finally released him—only to clutch him again.

"Don't cry. Don't cry," repeated the mantra in my head. It was futile. Though Daniel managed to keep his composure, tears rode down my cheek and trickled under my nose. Breaking away from me, Daniel turned and floated up the escalator. With mounting despair, I locked my eyes on his back, trying to memorize what might be my last glimpse.

He did not look back.

Son Mario tried to comfort me with a hug. My husband Mario recited all the reasons that Daniel would "be okay." My husband was appealing to the cerebral part of my brain, a tactic he may have found reassuring for himself, but which did not reassure me.

I cried nearly the entire trip home. Though Daniel was leaving to do a job that was dangerous and challenging, for him, there was also the thrill of adventure. He got to *do*. Mario and I could only wait—passive and helpless. There was nothing we could do to keep Daniel safe.

Of the two roles, Mario admitted it was far more difficult to be the parent than to be the warrior.

He confided guiltily, "I never thought about what my parents went through. A phone call from Vietnam was never an option, but I rarely wrote them a letter. My poor mom!"

The worst aspect of being left behind—especially for Mario—was the sense of impotence. Because a father feels responsible for his family's safety, it was particularly distressing to be unable to protect his son from harm.

There was another cause for his distress: he wanted to go to war too. He wanted to have the adventure and satisfaction of completing a mission. But especially he wanted to go to Iraq, in Daniel's place, so that *he* would be the one in harm's way rather than Daniel. Or, at the least, accompany Daniel to Iraq so that he could, by virtue of his prior experiences, keep Daniel safe.

For forty years Mario has carried the belief that the military never was allowed the opportunity to complete the job they knew they could do in Vietnam. It was his opinion that domestic political forces had prevented our military from winning. To be permitted to perform a mission "right" this time would have allowed him the opportunity to remove the tarnish that the Vietnam War was the only war which the public claimed had been "lost." Though Mario longed for another chance to make it right, he would have to stand on the sidelines instead and watch his son take on the mission.

Mario was in e-mail contact with his Marine Vietnam veteran brothers, and many of them wrote of the same feelings. Many felt they had lived enough of their lives that they would rather it be they who were killed in battle instead of these young men. Their e-mails frequently expressed frustration at being unable to have any useful role in the current conflict.

Since Vietnam vets were the largest group to have had recent experience in guerilla-style warfare they truly might have had some wisdom to offer.

Emotionally, they wanted to get in the fight too. For many, of course, that was not a possibility. As men in their late fifties and sixties, many had health issues that would have prevented them from any active participation. Nonetheless, there were some who were in as good a shape as some of the equally-older Army Reserve troops who were already serving in Iraq. I know Mario spent a lot of time searching for something he could do—even if he served in Iraq in a clerical capacity. He investigated being a contractor for support services there. He explored whether there was any way he could share his pearls of combat wisdom with Marines in training at Camp Pendleton. To be useful—especially if he could have had a combat role—might have allowed him some closure to his own war experience.

These feelings of being put on a shelf, as well as their own memories and feelings of rejection for participation in an unpopular war, took on a new life as these vets watched the current war in Iraq. This dynamic contributed to a reawakening, or ratcheting up, of pre-existing post-traumatic stress for many of them.

Mario commented, "I have learned that post-traumatic stress doesn't go away. It is always in the background. There isn't a day that I don't think about that time. But I realize I have to control it and not let it control me."

However, with events such as the first Gulf War and now this war, post-traumatic stress resurfaced. In Mario's situation I saw more moping, fury at world events and at many politicians, as well as avoidance of many social activities and people with opposite political viewpoints. Passions ran high with regard to the war; some people deliberately had confrontational dialogues with us. It was better and less painful to avoid those people. This was easier to do when they were social acquaintances. It was not always possible when they were family.

When Daniel returned to Camp Pendleton after his pre-deployment liberty, there were still two weeks before he left for Iraq. For me, the pain of saying goodbye at the airport was mitigated by the fact that, though I wouldn't be able to see him again, I was still able to speak with him by phone over the next ten days. That his departure had been broken into stages made it easier for me.

We wanted to go to Camp Pendleton to see him off, but he requested that we not come. My mind understood; my heart did not. Though watching him leave the base would have been more painful than our airport goodbye had been, I didn't want to pass up an opportunity to see him one more time. With reluctance I accepted that perhaps he didn't want to deal with our emotions; his own might have been all he could handle.

Chapter Twelve

2ND BATTALION 1ST MARINES
IRAQ DEPLOYMENT

Daniel phoned us on February 28 to say goodbye. He was at the battalion parade deck along with all the other Marines waiting for the bus to take them to March Air Force Base, where they would begin the journey to Iraq. I could hear lots of noise in the background—including the squeals of children. Daniel told me that while the Marines waited for the military buses, their children were running, playing, and jumping in a bounce house that had been set up for the families at 2/1's Camp Horno headquarters. I pictured little children saying goodbye to their daddies, and then I knew Daniel had been wise to discourage us from being there with him. That would have been too emotional a scene for me.

Daniel then mentioned that two of his cousins from the Bay Area and another cousin, stationed at an Air Force base nearby, were with him. They waited, all the while cracking jokes and laughing. I was envious that they could be there, but grateful for the light-hearted distraction they provided him. That was far better for him than the drama I likely would have provided.

For the first week or so that he was in the Middle East I knew he was relatively safe, off-loading vehicles in Kuwait. Publicly, I maintained a fairly calm veneer, but the sadness was always inside.

I continued to be involved with my Military Family Support Group, leading meetings monthly and e-mailing various members. One of the moms, Desi, lent me the red, white, and blue Swarovski crystal bracelet that someone had given her when her son was deployed to Iraq. It had become her good luck charm. Now that her son was safely home, she wanted me to wear it. (After Daniel came home from Iraq, Desi passed the bracelet to another mom in our group, Chris, who wore it when her sons were deployed to Iraq and Afghanistan.)

That summer, twelve sons of our approximately twenty-member group were in Iraq. The first meeting after Daniel left, I was pleasantly surprised that our daughter, no longer a teenager, and who had once declared the support group "lame," began to attend the meetings.

Mario had an opportunity to work full time in an accounting position at the University. The job offered diversion from worry while Daniel was in Iraq, and I strongly encouraged him to take it. Too much leisure time in the previous year had amplified his depression. Nonetheless, the culture of the University tended to be more liberal than Mario was able to tolerate. He did not initiate political conversations, but co-workers, presuming that listeners shared their views, felt free to do so. In order to maintain self-control during these election year political discussions, Mario gradually isolated himself more and more from co-workers during his breaks. Eventually, he felt so consummately alienated that, little more than two years later, he quit.

The week of March 11, I attended a professional conference in San Francisco. I had turned my cell phone off while I was in a lecture, and was distressed to later realize that I had missed a phone call from Daniel in Kuwait. Unable to reach either Mario or me on our cell phones, he left a voice message stating that he was leaving for Iraq with the rest of the battalion the next day. I was crushed that I had missed the chance to speak with him, but at least Daniel had been able to reach his brother Damián for a chat.

Knowing Daniel was traversing that very dangerous stretch of highway from Kuwait into Iraq, I began to repeat to myself the new mantra that Elizabeth suggested, "Thank you, God, for keeping my son safe for the past five minutes." Despite that exercise, I was still fearful. Over the weeks, I found myself calculating the time of day in Iraq and imagining what Daniel might be doing. I whispered encouragement and endearments, sending them energetically to him, while I tried not to worry that I hadn't heard from him since that last call from Kuwait.

The news from Fallujah was not encouraging. Within two days of the arrival of the approximately eight hundred Marines in 2/1 (who would soon relieve the Army's 82nd Airborne), the base outside Fallujah was mortared, causing injuries. The pace of insurgent attacks continued to pick up, and, less than a week after 2/1's arrival, two soldiers from the 82nd had been killed, fourteen soldiers and five Marines were injured in action—twice the number of deaths and one-fifth the number of injured than the Army's 82nd Airborne had experienced during their entire tour in Fallujah.

For two weeks following the arrival of 2/1, the 82nd Airborne stayed and performed joint patrols with the Marines to allow the newcomers to acclimate to their new duties. On March 25, responsibility for the town of Fallujah—as well as the surrounding area—passed from the 82nd Airborne to the 2nd Battalion, 1st Marines, under the command of Lt. Col. Gregg Olson.

It would seem that the Iraqis were wily enough to exploit the fact that there were new troops. Images of firefights in the town were televised in America.

The original intent was to have a "velvet glove" approach with the Iraqis (this attitude was summarized as the famous "no better friend, no worse enemy"). This meant Marines would help residents reestablish their infrastructure, and perform humanitarian projects, such as health care. Fallujah still contained many members of Sadaam Hussein's Baath party who were hostile to American interests. There had been much insurgent activity in the town from the moment the Marines arrived. Once in charge, the Marines launched an offensive against insurgents, who had been acting with impunity against the Americans, even purportedly using a mosque as an armory. The Marines began to sweep the town to root out the insurgents. On March 26, the first Marine from 2/1, PFC Leroy Sandoval, was killed in action.

On March 29, we got a brief note from Daniel:

> Hi. Sorry I haven't been able to write or call, but we've
> been busy. The place where we're staying [Camp Volturno,

which was renamed Camp Baharia, was two miles southeast of Fallujah] has a crazy history. It used to be a Baath party resort, so it's really nice with a lake in it. Sadaam and his kids, Ude and Kuze [sic] had their houses here. They used to kidnap women out in Fallujah and bring them here and rape and torture them. It's kind of sad. The drive up here wasn't too bad. Now that we're here, things have been crazy. We get mortar-attacked everyday, and if you go out in town, it's guaranteed that you'll be shot at with RPGs [rocket-propelled grenades]. Now they've got me on guard duty which kind of sucks, but at night you get a front row seat for the mortar attacks…

When, on the last day in March, a party of American contractors was ambushed, murdered, and their burned bodies suspended over the highway, there was pressure for the Americans to put aside the velvet glove and provide a strong military response. Apparently against their wishes, Marine commanders were given an order to begin an offensive on Fallujah, known as Operation Vigilant Resolve. As 2/1 entered a sector of the city, intense firefights erupted—one battle even lasting thirty-six hours.

With military operations came casualties, both military and civilian, which sparked a political *pas de deux* between local and Coalition administrators. In the end, though the Marines had surrounded Fallujah and were ready to close in on insurgents, they were ordered to begin a unilateral ceasefire.

Marines were frustrated; their perception was that they were only a few days short of clearing Fallujah of insurgents and achieving control of the city. Instead, they were pulled up short by pressure from politicians here at home. They grumbled that the ceasefire would only allow insurgents the time and freedom to augment their weapons stockpiles and fortify the town, enabling it to be a locus from which terrorist acts could be plotted and executed with impunity. Regrettably, that assessment turned out to be correct.

Throughout the month of April insurgent attacks on Marines resulted in considerable numbers of dead and wounded.

I was getting ready for work one April morning while listening to a television news program in another room. Suddenly I became aware of sounds of yelling and gunfire. I ran to see live film footage of Marines in Fallujah shooting from rooftops and bellowing instructions to their men. I imagined how frightened these young men might be—even though their adrenalin rush was likely thrilling. As I watched that scene, I started to unravel. The helmets and goggles that the Marines wore made it difficult to identify a specific Marine. What if one of them was Daniel?

I decided that being a remote eyewitness was an unnerving modern innovation, and, from that moment on, I would no longer get my news from television. Daniel's tour had only just started; how would I be able to endure six more months of this?

There were days when the news from Fallujah was so grim I held my breath when I turned down our street after work, and burst into tears of relief that no car with Marines in dress blues waited for me.

I found it distressing that strangers, co-workers, friends, and even family, spewed political opinions on me, and even on strangers who were silently standing in a grocery line or in quiet conversation with a friend.

On one occasion, while at the gym in the spring of 2004, a man I didn't know nodded towards my Marine tee-shirt and asked if my son was "over there." When I answered in the affirmative, his next comment was "Well, you know that we shouldn't be over there, don't you?" Gee, was that comment supposed to make me feel better? To him, such discussion was an intellectual exercise. To me, it was my child! This man's comment gave me the feeling that, were anything to happen to my son, he would just shrug, as if to imply that Daniel had asked for it.

I was accosted nearly daily by people who would ask how Daniel was. If only they would have stopped there. Instead, too often they launched into a monologue of their opinion regarding the justification for war, the conduct of the war, or the President. Though I refrained, I wanted to say, "Oh, *excuse me!* I thought this was about my son. I get it now. This is really about *you* and your opinions."

A co-worker told me that the war was stupid and it was stupid my son had been sent to Iraq. I knew most of these people never meant to be hurtful. In fact, they assumed I must be bitter about my son being at war and believed they were in solidarity with me. Yet, it pained me to think that if Daniel were killed in Iraq someone would think it was all "stupid." People asked political questions or asked about my views of the war, but when I replied that I really did not want to get into such a discussion I was admonished that I ought to be able to be open to an exchange of ideas. I know people were truly curious, but I found their insistence threatening to my delicately-poised emotions.

I didn't see myself as definitely one side or another; but we were already in Iraq and could only go forward from that point. While my son was deployed, I felt I did not have the luxury of doubting the wisdom or value of my son's mission. I made efforts to wall myself off from remarks that threatened my own calm. People's inept and boorish comments made me want to avoid them.

My emotions were mercurial, a fickleness to which I was unaccustomed. Both sad and happy events now caused me to be emotional. Sometimes anguish for Daniel's safety was so strong that even thinking of him would cause me to tear up. There were times I would cry reading positive, uplifting e-mails about our troops or their families. There were times when people would tell me to thank Daniel for his service, and I was so touched that I could scarcely mumble "thanks."

Mario still watched a lot of television news when he got home from work. He sometimes became furious at the comments of talk show guests. He cursed them and sometimes stomped angrily through the house, complaining loudly about them. He didn't sleep well most nights, though a contributing factor was that he was in need of a knee replacement. He also slept a lot during the days when he was not at work. It was obvious to me that he was depressed. He didn't deny it; he just felt that the only cure was having his son return safely from deployment. He didn't see the need to seek counseling till much later when I told him how difficult it was for me to keep my own spirits from sinking as a result of his dark moods and explosive tantrums regarding things over which neither of us had control.

As in the previous year, Mario again found it difficult to socialize. He tried to force himself to attend some social functions, but his heart wasn't in it. He had little tolerance for situations that required superficial chitchat. As happened the previous year, he would agree to attend a function, and then, more often than not, cancel just when it was time to leave the house.

As before, he didn't feel he could party "as long as Daniel is in Iraq." If he did actually attend an event, he usually seemed to have a good time. Then he felt guilty when he did have fun, all of which only reinforced his tendency to isolate. More and more, I became his only social outlet.

Which brings me to another, more delicate, topic. Sexual intimacy suffered during this time as well. To different degrees, we each found it difficult to "be in the mood." Though our logical brains told us that we need not feel guilty for seeking the temporary pleasant distraction and healing that intimacy offered, our emotional brains could not get past feeling such pleasures were inappropriately self-indulgent perhaps at the very moment when our son might be in danger. That is not to say there was no love life; rather, it was distinctly curtailed. This is one of the less-acknowledged consequences of deployment. Though people seldom speak of these issues, I know some other military parents have similar experiences.

Now that Daniel was in Iraq, my new morning routine was to race to the computer immediately upon awakening to see if there was an e-mail from Daniel. Next, I looked at online newspaper articles written by those reporters embedded with 2/1. Over the seven months, three different newspapers had placed embedded reporters with various companies in Daniel's unit. I would scan the headlines and then go to the *New York Times* Web site. Usually my anxiety level could tolerate only a few paragraphs for each news item. After that, I spent the early morning hours in prodigious e-mail correspondence.

Then, there was the afternoon routine, which entailed checking the Department of Defense press releases each day for the names of military persons killed in Iraq or Afghanistan, in case there was a name I recognized— which had happened. I would also check the "Military Photos of the Day" on the Web site for the *Marine Corps Times*, looking for possible photos of Daniel (I never found one of Daniel, though I did see some photos of others I knew).

On March 31, I sent out an e-mail to my growing list of interested friends and family:

> I wanted to let you know I *finally* heard from Daniel at 2:30 this morning. He had just gotten back from a big operation

in Fallujah. He said the Marines will probably go out daily to try to secure the town. The large firefight last Friday was an effort to secure what had been the most dangerous intersection in Fallujah and which he deemed was now secured.... He got back early from the operation and he had some leisure and [not much] wait time to open his e-mail for the first time since he'd arrived. They have been mostly sleeping and working.

The connection was quite good—clear and without the satellite delay. Because of the time of day he called [Depending on whether it was Daylight Savings Time or not, Iraq was either 10 or 11 hours ahead of Pacific Time] hardly anyone was using the phones, and so we spoke for 30 minutes. He had gotten the first set of packages I'd mailed three weeks ago—with sweet tarts, gummy worms and other non-melting candy for Easter. I had sent him enough for him to share, and he said everyone was eating it. Where he is there is no shortage of hand sanitizer, but will share the ones I sent him when he gets it. Currently he is living in a small house with about 20 others from H & S. They get along pretty well. There is a TV and a DVD player in his house. He...wants us to send him *Schindler's List* and some other DVDs.

One person in their group had brought his play station and it arrived unscathed, so all of the Marines are enjoying using it.

He is already thinking ahead to the time he returns from the deployment—five months from now...

We had a hard time sleeping after talking to our boy!

Daniel called us on a satellite phone on April 10. When the firefights started, he had been taken off guard duty so that he could participate in operations in Fallujah. As usual, I sent out a group e-mail to our friends:

> Daniel just called. He said he was at the base, but about to head out to Fallujah again (it's 10 pm on Saturday there). He was back at the base during the cease-fire, but otherwise has been in Fallujah. He is mostly just driving everyone and every thing in any vehicle. He sometimes has to do "infantry things" (whatever that means)…During the conversation there was mortaring in the background. He stopped to listen at one point to hear how close it was. In my own inexperienced opinion, I thought it was close; it sounded like a huge package had dropped off a desk next to him.…
>
> We talked for three or four minutes before he needed to go. At least I had time to tell him we loved him, and at least I know that, up till now, whatever I've heard on the news doesn't pertain to him. I am very worried, though, about the hostility level in Fallujah being so high right now that he is at risk even more as he heads into town.
>
> You Vietnam vets from 2/1, thank you for your encouraging letter to the current Marines of 2/1. I know you know how much that means to have the previous generation be supportive and confident of the current troops. Thank you for all the e-mails and your prayers. Some days we are very discouraged and your words of encouragement from those who have "been there" mean a lot to us.
>
> Thanks, everyone, so much for your prayers. They are keeping us afloat. It means a lot to me. And, Cheryl, I like your image of wrapping Daniel in a blanket of prayer. All

of you in my Chico Military Family Support Group and in the 2/1 vet family…are in our prayers every day.

When Daniel left for Iraq, I had made sure that the battalion's Family Readiness Officer (FRO) had my e-mail address. The FRO stays behind when the battalion deploys and among other duties acts as the point of contact between the unit's deployed officers and the families at home. The FRO for 2/1 transmitted the occasional official updates from the commanders in Iraq to the families. In the first weeks of the deployment, his e-mails contained the e-mail addresses of eight or so other recipients who were family members of Marines in 2/1. I looked at the names and addresses at the top of each e-mail and debated whether I should e-mail those others so we could "talk" electronically to each other. While I hesitated out of propriety, one of the other addressees broke the ice. With this dad's e-mail, an informal electronic support group was born.

Over the weeks, more and more families' names were added to the mailing list. By the last month of the deployment, there were approximately forty persons on the list. Not everyone chose to participate in the round-robin of our e-mail chatter; some preferred to write only occasionally. Nevertheless, I believe it became a wonderful source of support for most of us to hear from those whose Marines were on the same mission. As we began to e-mail each other, we found we became family. We shared what information we'd gleaned when our Marines called or e-mailed. We laughed with each other, sent each other uplifting messages, encouraged each other, and cried with each other. I have always suspected that the FRO intentionally left the e-mail addresses on his communications in the hope that we would do exactly what we did do—that is, take care of each other. This became the parental version of "foxhole" friendships.

I still keep in contact with several of my online 2/1 families. Even though I have never met most of these wonderful people, it doesn't matter; these are friends of the heart.

The president of the Vietnam Veterans of the 2nd Battalion, 1st Marines sent the following letter of support to the commanders of 2/1 in Fallujah as well as to the 2/1 infantry Marines in Iraq:

April 6, 2004

My Fellow Marines:

It cannot be said too often: You are the future of this nation! Once again our young people are being charged with the responsibility to guard the gate to our nation's freedom! And whether the world likes it or not, you are undertaking this battle for all of mankind's right to exist free of oppression and terror.

As we before you, and those before us, those who pick up arms for our country to fight for our freedoms, are challenged to succeed under harsh and unfriendly circumstances. Your enemy will have different names and languages than our enemies did, but they will be defeated by you. And toward that end we stand united with you.

Your mission is one that is being witnessed by the world and your mission has no option but to succeed. We, your brothers of the Vietnam Veterans of 2nd Battalion 1st Marines stand behind you in this endeavor. We stand united in supporting you and your families, and want you to know that the American people remember you each day, in their prayers and thoughts.

Fight hard and use the skills the Marine Corps has trained you with. These skills kept many of us alive during the Vietnam War. Stand together and fight for each other, knowing that there is no greater honor than being a United States Marine. As we watch the news reports each day, we are proud to have you carry our colors into combat. Your names have joined the ranks of our past heroes, and your efforts will be etched in our hearts and minds forever.

God's speed!

On behalf of all the Vietnam Veterans of 2nd Bn 1st Marines, we salute you!

Thomas A. Matteo, President
SSgt. USMC Fox 2/1 1968-69

I was touched by this gesture of support, knowing how significant it was for these Vietnam veterans to give the support that they themselves had never received to the new generation of Marines.

Mario's 2/1 Vietnam veteran friends frequently e-mailed us to find out about Daniel and to check on us. Some also sent care packages to the 2/1 Marines in Iraq. Some even "adopted" wounded Marines, writing them notes and sending them care packages. And many reminded us in their letters that Daniel was on the prayer lists at their various churches as well as in their own daily prayers.

Keeping up with the volume of e-mail communication became a bit daunting at times. It was not unusual that, between my hometown support group and my 2/1 families, I might spend two or three hours a day on the computer. An amazing evolution since two years before I was too terrified of the computer to even turn it on. E-mailing also served the purpose of channeling a lot of my nervous energy as well. The downside was that I stayed up late many nights trying to keep connected with the others, lend an electronic ear, and offer validation and support. E-mailing allowed me to connect in an immediate way with so many more people than geographical distances would have permitted otherwise. And it provided an opportunity to put my own fears aside and do something helpful for others.

After each phone call from Daniel, I sent out "Daniel Updates" to my hometown support group, the Vietnam vets, as well as many friends and family. My "Update" mailing list probably included, by the end of the deployment, close to eighty persons. Networking in this way certainly connected me to so many others that, despite the time commitment the e-mail correspondence took, this heart-to-heart connection nurtured me.

In a group e-mail I sent on April 16, I noted:

Daniel called last night. He was able to use the satellite phone because, being in the convoy's lead car, he has access to it. He was doing okay—just busy driving all the time. He had been able to sleep on the base the last two nights, which was a relief, but he said that would probably change soon. He said they are rotating guys periodically back to the base from the town of Fallujah so they can be "breaked." I asked him if the road from the base to the town was safe. He said "yes" because the town is just outside the base gate. It's going into the center of town that is unsafe. There are always attacks on the Marines with every foray into town....

He mentioned that 2/1, having been in Iraq the previous year, had requested a lot of specific supplies based on their earlier experience and so they were well-stocked with necessary supplies.... [One company] was stationed on the Euphrates [a distance from the Forward Operating Base]. A few days ago Daniel and other drivers had been loaded with supplies to take to this other company. As they headed out the base gate, they were called and told to return to base, as the road they would be traveling was too dangerous. Daniel was irritated until he found out later that a row of about fifteen IEDs was strewn in the road and the entire convoy would have been destroyed.

Daniel says mostly he drives or he sleeps. He spends long days driving and gets little sleep. Occasionally he mans a machine gun. There is a chance he may get assigned to Fox Company (which is involved heavily with all the sh— going on). Since [the first firefight] Fox has lost quite a few men and may want to replace with new guys.

Over the course of his deployment, it was not unusual for Daniel to call just before he headed out of the base for several days of patrol. While I never minded his 2:00 AM phone calls, I did find it extremely difficult to fall asleep afterward if he told us he was headed out on patrol for the next few days. It meant that I knew he was in danger *while* he was in danger. Very eerie. My anxiety was never gone.

Daniel called several more times during the last week of April. He said he'd gone into Fallujah daily. The Marines had never stopped patrolling, but since things had been a bit quieter the previous few weeks, the Marines had ventured deeper into the town. He himself had been in Fallujah for the past several days. Sometimes he slept in buildings and, when there was a watch posted, sometimes in the Humvees. I wondered if he was exhausted from the constant tension, but he replied, "You get used to it. There's nothing you can do about it anyway."

In a later phone call Daniel mentioned casually that around Easter time he had been the target of a sniper while he was driving the lead vehicle. "Well, I'm glad you had a bullet-proof windshield!" I commented. He replied that the shooter hadn't hit the window.

"Then how great you had a vehicle with bullet-proof doors," I offered.

"Mom, he didn't shoot the door either."

"I don't understand. Where did the bullet hit?" I asked.

"The bullet landed in the roof of the car just a few inches above my head," he replied.

Trying to make sure that I sounded calm, perhaps even breezy, so that he wouldn't think he could never tell me any scary details of his experiences, I merely commented, "Well, it's good that he missed!"

Daniel told his sister in a later phone call that, immediately following that incident, a Marine sniper had been dispatched to find the Iraqi shooter and to "take care" of him, which the Marine apparently did. It still gives me the creeps to think of Daniel's close call.

I am squeamish thinking that someone hunted down the Iraqi shooter. Killing a person who is trying to kill you during combat is an easier notion to me than stalking and later detachedly killing him. Nonetheless, I am not judgmental of the sniper's role. I am glad that the Iraqi shooter missed

Daniel, and I confess I was relieved that he was permanently unable to kill someone else's son.

Daniel's care package requests were for CDs, protein shakes, Gatorade, or fruit punch powders—because "the MREs [Meals Ready to Eat] are getting old"—as well as packs of soccer trading cards that he could hand out to Iraqi children.

One time I asked Daniel how troop morale was. He said it was pretty good—"considering." When I asked for clarification, he said, "Considering we'd rather not be here."

In May Mario's father died. He'd suffered some health problems in the previous two months, and died in Guatemala of an apparent heart attack. We had to wait for a week or so till Daniel called us to be able to inform him. He handled the news well. I had worried that he might be very upset, but I think his world was so precarious that there was little room to focus on anything but his own situation.

The week after Mario's father died, Daniel called us and told us that one of the Humvees had gone over an IED a few days before, killing a Marine in Fox Company. He didn't know the Marine who had been killed, but he did know some of the ones who were injured. Marines in the field are prohibited from naming those who are injured or killed until the information has become public. This policy is rarely breached, but there have been instances of family members learning of a loved one's death or injury from informal conversation before a bereavement team can give the official notification in person.

A few days after I spoke with Daniel, I was scrolling the new Department of Defense press releases for those killed in action, when I saw a name, PFC Brandon Sturdy, that I recognized as being the son of one of our e-mail group's very active participants. And one of those injured in the same blast was a son from our e-mail group as well. My heart dropped to my shoes. I set about double-checking my information, but, unfortunately, it was true. It was, of course, the nightmare all parents dread. And now it had happened to parents in our online 2/1 group.

For Mario the death of a Marine packed a one-two punch. As a parent he grieved the loss of this young man. And, as a Marine, he mourned the loss of a "brother." For all of us, it underscored the reality that this could just as easily have been our son.

One of Mario's 2/1 Vietnam vet friends, Tom ("Stormy") Matteo, himself wounded six times in Vietnam, wrote me:

> Mario is faced with first-hand knowledge [of] what it means to lose one of our own. Marines don't take this lightly and we have a personal relationship with each man who may pass on. We also have the guilt feeling that we should have been there and maybe we could have done something to change this [outcome].

As the then-president of the Vietnam Veterans of 2/1, Tom was very active on behalf of the Iraq 2/1 Marines. He sent care packages to the 2/1 Marines in Iraq and sent Marine Corps blankets to the families in Daniel's unit whose sons were KIA (Killed In Action). Others in the veterans' group also sent care packages to Marines in the field. When information about those who are Wounded In Action (WIA) was obtained, some of the vets who lived close to the military hospitals made efforts to visit the injured. Others sent get-well cards.

Several parents in our 2/1 e-mail group became aware of two Marines who didn't seem to be receiving any mail. They e-mailed an appeal to our group to write these Marines. Our 2/1 e-mail group, as well as my local military support group, began to flood these Marines with mail and care packages. I was truly touched by the outpouring of love and kindness.

Interestingly, one of the two pieces of hand-written mail from Daniel during his entire Iraq deployment was a three-line note saying: "Dear Mom and Dad, They made me write a letter to you. The battalion has to. Talk to you later on the phone. Love, Daniel."

Apparently there had been a spate of communication from parents to the commanders in the field, inquiring about the welfare of their Marines since they had not heard from their sons in quite awhile. Mario and I had to laugh when we read Daniel's obligatory letter. We were fortunate that Daniel managed to e-mail or call every two to three weeks. Daniel has since told us that phoning was a very arduous process. Using the base phones might mean waiting in line for an hour or more in the hot sun. Since he had only one day off, Daniel often chose to sleep, or he chose to e-mail rather than phone, since the wait for a computer was likely to be only thirty to forty-five minutes.

Once in a while, when he went out on patrol, Daniel was able to call us from the Command Post's satellite phone. In an interesting turn of events, one of the persons to whom he once lent the sat-phone was his former boot camp drill instructor, assigned to the same battalion as Daniel. Now that Daniel was no longer a lowly recruit, he and his former drill instructor developed a friendship.

I found a way to indirectly check Daniel's welfare. Because I had set up his e-mail account years before, I knew his password. He had asked me to go through his e-mail periodically to delete the Spam before it used up all the space on his account. I never opened his e-mail letters (tempting as it sometimes was), but I could also at least see if he'd used his computer recently. If my latest e-mail to him was flagged as already opened or in the "delete" file, then I knew that, as of the date of his last opened e-mail, Daniel had been well. Even if he hadn't e-mailed us when he had used the computer, it was a relief to realize he was okay.

In the beginning of June, our daughter Clarissa became a volunteer for Camp Adventure, a program for dependents on our military bases and embassies. She eventually volunteered with this program for three summers in a row, traveling to Tokyo, Okinawa, Beijing, and Madrid. That summer Clarissa was assigned to Japan to teach swimming to dependents at a US. Naval base near Tokyo. It was a wonderfully rich opportunity. I was excited for her, but it was very hard to now have two children so far away. Ironically, Daniel was the nearer of the two, being *only* ten time zones away, whereas Clarissa was sixteen time zones away

I was pretty emotional for the remainder of the day when Clarissa left for Japan. When we went out to eat later that night, I dissolved in tears of relief when Daniel called while we were eating.

He said it was pretty boring when he wasn't working (there was nothing wrong with "boring" as far as I was concerned). There had been several days when the temperature was 118°. A friend, with whom he had served in 1st FAST, was a squad leader in the 3rd Platoon of Fox Company (Mario's company and platoon) and wanted Daniel to try to arrange a transfer to his squad. Between deaths and injuries, Fox Company had lost quite a few Marines, and Daniel would be a welcome combat replacement. He told us that when he transferred to Fox, he would be the Squad Automatic Weapon (SAW), or M249, gunner for his squad. Ideally, a squad consists of three four-man "fire teams" plus the squad leader, and a Navy corpsman; however, by the end of the tour, due to deaths, injuries, and illnesses, many squads did not have the full complement of personnel.

Daniel worked diligently for several weeks to facilitate a reassignment and finally received word that he would be moving to Fox Company, 3rd Platoon in June. Mario was thrilled that his son would be in *his* company and platoon.

In the middle of June, my father-in-law's funeral became the occasion for a huge family reunion. Sons Mario and Damián and Damián's wife Katie accompanied us to Guatemala. Since Katie had never visited Guatemala, we took advantage of our ten days there to do some sightseeing. We enjoyed the trip and it was fun to see Katie enjoying the country and culture.

Because of our busy travel schedule, I had irregular e-mail access and little exposure to news. In fact, it was a rather eerie feeling to be in a location where the war in Iraq was almost a non-event. I found it frustrating to have so little information when I was anxious for news from the front.

On the few occasions I was able to visit an Internet café, I combed the military Web sites. That was when I learned a Marine had gone missing in Iraq. I worried about the young Marine and what the enemy might do to him. When it was reported that a group in Iraq had threatened to behead him, I was agitated. A few weeks later I learned that the "kidnapping" might have been an elaborately-staged ruse. How far-reaching the ramifications a stranger's action can have. I'm sure I was one of many persons who literally lost sleep over him—for nothing, it would seem.

About the same time, I learned from a news Web site that there had been a major fight on June 24, in which eight Marines were wounded, on the cloverleaf of the main highway leading into Fallujah. One of the mothers in our 2/1 e-mail group—a woman with whom I felt a strong bond—informed me that her son, Sgt. Andrew K. Parker, had been seriously wounded in that firefight. He had been shot in the leg, the bones shattered. The doctors had advised a leg amputation, but he refused. He was told he might not walk again. He vowed instead that, not only would he walk again, he would run. Despite multiple surgeries, infections, and a year of recovery, this resolute and courageous Marine eventually ran six-minute miles, finished a marathon, and deployed for three more tours with another unit. His sheer grit and determination continues to inspire my awe and admiration.

At the time of the firefight at the cloverleaf, Daniel had been in Fox Company, 3rd Platoon for only a few weeks. Months later he wrote a report about that day:

> Our platoon was the battalion quick reaction force for that week. We responded to a huge attack on Golf Company early in the morning at the cloverleaf. We pulled up in the seven-ton trucks and hopped off to find rounds pinging off the 7-ton and little clouds of dust popping up all around us from where the insurgents' rounds were impacting [and] trying to shoot us, as well as feeling the whiz and hearing that distinct loud snap of rounds hitting inches away from our face.

> We ran up to the top of the cloverleaf to get some cover and returned fire into the buildings. Every few minutes our fire team had to keep running to the other side of the cloverleaf, each time running under the overpass, fully exposed and silhouetted for the insurgents to take shots at us. Each round narrowly missed and it felt as if they were circling us with rounds. Every few minutes, convoys left with casualties. Tanks, 2nd LAR [Light Armored Reconnaissance] and air power came to our rescue until a Super Cobra helicopter was shot down about a hundred feet to our front. We were told that we were going to have to secure the crash site, but [another company did instead]. There never seemed to be a dull moment. Rounds continued to whiz past us and RPGs and mortars were being shot at us. More casualties were evacuated out of there. Then my fire team ran to the

other side of the cloverleaf again. When we ran under the overpass an RPG flew right between me and another Marine. I decided that I wasn't going to run under it again if I could help it. We kept returning fire and killed several insurgents, including those wearing desert utilities and who we figured were Iraq Civil Defense Corps runaways. We were then told to run to the other side. This time it was an entire squad. We bounded and ran under the overpass again and heard a sharp, loud noise that we [couldn't] figure out. It was so strong and painful to our ears that the lance corporal that I was with and I both fell. But we had to quickly get up because the shooting from the insurgents would not let up; we ran to the other side. By this time it was late afternoon. The firing finally began to slow down and tanks began to egress the area. We were told altogether there were about 17 casualties from Golf Company and we had killed more than 100 insurgents. I have no idea how accurate that is. That was the longest steady firefight I have ever been in. It lasted hours and never seemed to let up.

Daniel has told me the outdoor temperature that day was unusually hot, even for an Iraqi summer day. The air temperature was 140°. However, the Marines were fighting on an asphalt road, which retained the heat. One Marine's watch contained a thermometer feature, which measured the air temperature on the cloverleaf asphalt as 160°. Since the men necessarily wore heavy bullet-resistant vests and helmets, I asked Daniel if many Marines suffered problems with the heat. Daniel was unaware of any heat casualties in his particular platoon, likely due to the officers' repeated commands to drink water. With all the perspiration these Marines had to be producing, I couldn't begin to fathom the liters and liters of water it would have taken to keep the men hydrated—or the numbers of empty plastic water bottles that must have been piling up around them.

Daniel didn't call while we were in Guatemala, so I did not learn any of these details of the eight-hour fight till he called home on July 5.

Since the firefight on the cloverleaf, he'd been out on patrol until the Fourth of July. He was at the base for one day only and would be "back in the saddle" again the following morning. He had been a SAW gunner when he first got to Fox, but he now carried a different weapon—a rifle with a scope. I made the observation that he was no longer driving others in Humvees; someone was now driving *him*. His response was it was nice when he wasn't the driver because he didn't have to worry about all the guys in the back of his vehicle. I suddenly realized how much pressure he must have been under all these months: the worry that he might not see a danger in the road and might drive over an IED, the guilt he would carry if something happened to his friends while he was driving.

We chatted a bit about the weather. Daniel said it was very hot in the daytime and in the 90's in the evening, which now felt chilly to the men. I recalled that one of the support group moms had reported her son lying in bed, shivering in his sleeping bag, when the nighttime temperature dipped to 90°.

Morale was "pretty good," which was amazing to me, given the heat, no days off, and the increase in casualties.

Before Daniel hung up, he mentioned that someone from Fox Company had died the day before. When the Department of Defense released the name, it was again someone whose parents were in our 2/1-e-mail group. In this instance, their Marine apparently had been killed in a vehicle accident rather than due to hostile action. By the end of the deployment, I estimate that nearly twenty-five percent of the Marines whose families were in our Iraq 2/1 e-mail group had been killed or wounded. Some injuries were minor, only needing small amounts of time to recuperate in the theater of operations before returning to their units. Others had been injured significantly, and were flown stateside for treatment, in some cases requiring months of recuperation. One of those wounded was from the Chico area and his foster mother not only belonged to the 2/1-e-mail group but to our support group in Chico as well. Members of the Iraq 2/1-e-mail group, Mario's 2/1 Vietnam veterans group, as well as our local support group, wrote this foster mother to offer comfort. The young Marine recovered well and eventually rejoined the unit when it next deployed to Iraq.

During that summer, one of the members of our local group schemed to surprise the rest of us with something special. Sue belonged to a quilt guild whose members designed and stitched a different patriotic quilt for each military person in our support group. Five guild women, several of whom I did not know and have never met, worked for four months to stitch more than twenty quilts for our sons.

During the July support group meeting, this woman and her husband beautifully displayed each member's quilt over all the railing and wall space available throughout their home. Daniel's quilt had his name as well as a poem about the Marine Corps on the back. When all of us were tense with anxiety for our military child, those gestures of appreciation were heartening.

One soldier, home on R&R, found the quilt such a comfort that, rather than leaving it home for safekeeping, he insisted on taking it back to Iraq. Another soldier, who had been grieving over the violent death of a close friend at the hands of the enemy, found healing in the realization that people who didn't even know him had wanted to do something nice for him.

I still struggled with anxiety. My attention still strayed even from pleasurable activities. I found that when I started an activity, before I knew it, my attention had wandered. As there was a high volume of e-mail from people who wanted to know how Daniel was, I found myself popping up and down constantly to check the computer. Because I have a tendency to cope maladaptively with stress by eating, I also started to put on weight. When I observed how other parents in my hometown group handled their deployment stress, I found them inspirational. These parents modeled a tensile strength, fortifying my own coping ability. Their courage helped me to find my own.

I had been corresponding with the wife of Pete, one of Mario's newly found platoon buddies from Vietnam. Their son was deployed with the Army in Afghanistan. I confided to her some of the spiritual concerns Daniel's deployment provoked:

> I keep hoping that I will feel if Daniel's in need. If something happened to him, surely I would feel it? I don't know if I

will, or if I've already missed some big things. I just say little prayers and send him love throughout the day.

I was worried that, because I wasn't feeling serene, I might not have adequate faith. I have come to feel that, deep in my heart—despite my anxiety—I do believe in an unemotional yet convicted way, that God hears me. That he is taking care of Daniel in whatever way he knows is right for him. Even if it's *that*. The fact that I can't feel calm speaks more of my humanity. Just last week, I came to the awareness that I may not always be given the Consolation (in its Ignatian sense) of calm and serenity. Perhaps God withholds the gift of Consolation as a way of purifying my soul.

One of my favorite sayings is by St. Julie Billiart, the foundress of the Sisters of Notre Dame de Namur—the order that ran my high school in D.C.—"You must char the wood ere you can limn [draw] with it." The thought of my challenges being in fact the means to purify my soul *is* consoling.

My error/sin is to expect Consolation and then allowing the lack of same to cause me to doubt my faith. Anxiety is my personal cross, but I don't have to believe that my anxiety defines reality or me. My faith is deep enough that I can let all the emotions swirl at the surface and not attach myself to my emotions, but instead, dip deep into the well of my being and meet God there—regardless of all the fretting and worrying, which are my human weaknesses at the surface. Those I offer to God for healing. Don't know if that makes sense....

In a later e-mail I commented, "This deployment is one of the hardest things I have had to endure. About the only thing I can think of that would be worse is having a child die."

My husband had his own pain; he wrote in the online guest book for his 2/1 Vietnam veterans' Web site:

> How did our parents survive this agony? My Marine, Daniel, has been gone five months already and it has been pure hell. 24-7.... Thanks for your prayers and support. My wife and I will always be grateful. Daniel says he has received letters and e-mails from some of you. God bless you!

Mario felt tremendous guilt to think his parents must have felt just as he was feeling now, while he hadn't given serious thought to their pain.

By early August, Daniel was sending us a number of e-mails about things he wanted when he got home. He had already looked online at the prices of new and used cars, as well as looking into possible living quarters when he eventually moved back to Chico the following year.

On August 2, the tentative "window" of time for the battalion's homecoming was announced by the FRO: October 3 through 9. However, instead of being relieved that his return date was getting closer, we became more anxious. He was so close to the end of his tour, we couldn't bear something happening to him now. We were almost afraid to discuss any homecoming plans for fear of jinxing them. Not an unfounded fear, as it turned out.

We got an e-mail from him on August 5. Below, I have woven the e-mail with an account he wrote later to offer a more complete picture:

> Hi. I don't know if they gave you any news about the latest IED [we had heard nothing], but I was hit by one yesterday. Nobody was hurt. We were on patrol in our humvee. We were driving down a canal road outside of Saclawiyah (outside Fallujah) to do scheduled mounted patrol. We just passed about twenty to thirty kids swimming in the stream alongside the canal road. After we passed them, they scattered and ran off. I was driving the second humvee. My A-driver mentioned that it was a nice day. Instantly, I said

that I didn't have a good feeling; I thought we were going to get hit. He agreed, and not two seconds later, there was a huge explosion just behind me. The concussion and force made my ears lose their hearing [apparently the concussion caused everyone's eardrums to rupture]; and my ears began to ring. The blast lifted up my humvee but didn't flip it. Debris and shrapnel came falling down on me, since our humvee was topless. I was shaken and had trouble opening the door. When the corpsman opened it for me, my legs [were weak]. When I got [out], I saw that no one had been killed. Two shots from an AK-47 rang out, which I didn't hear at all [he was still deafened], but I was told the shots came from 20 feet away. After we secured the area, we didn't locate the shooter. I did find huge pieces of shrapnel lying on the ground about 9 inches long, 3 inches wide, and ¾ inch thick, with jagged edges which were still hot. EOD [Explosive Ordinance Disposal] came to the conclusion that the bomb was two 122-mm artillery rounds and a 155-artillery round daisy-chained. It was a pretty good explosion, heard miles away. It had hit about 5 feet behind my humvee. Somehow, no one was hurt; we were lucky not to be dead. Maybe it's because of the Jesus picture dad gave me and [the rosary] I have.

He gave the holy card way too much power, from my point of view. I believed it was the power of the prayers of countless people that kept him safe. I thanked God that my son was still alive.

On the surface, I was pretty matter-of-fact about the incident, but, inside, I was shaken to the core to realize how close we came to losing Daniel.

In mid-August, Mario and I traveled to Hawaii to meet our daughter as she returned from Japan. She had planned to spend the next academic year as an exchange student at the University of Hawaii in Hilo. She had only thirty-six jet-lagged hours to buy textbooks, linens, and kitchenware and to set up her apartment before classes began. She needed our help—not to mention our wallet. Besides, we hadn't seen her for two months and missed her.

Since we were going to be in Hawaii anyway, Mario and I opted for a romantic getaway on the western side of the Big Island a few days before we were to meet Clarissa. It never occurred to me to check whether the condos had air conditioning. Because the island is tropical, I assumed it was a given. But since the western side of the island is usually cooled by trade winds, it turns out that air conditioning is often optional. As luck would have it, the weather was unusually warm and humid. Worse, the ever-present trade winds were not blowing either.

When Mario and I entered our rental, we nearly suffocated from the stagnant hot air. We reminded ourselves often throughout the next few days, that the heat and humidity we experienced were minor compared to what Daniel was enduring. Even now I am embarrassed that we weren't even half as tough as our son; we left for Hilo—where our motel there had air conditioning—days before we'd planned. I had thought I was tough. Apparently not.

Even in "paradise" there was no relief from worry, and after Daniel's close call with the IED, we had even more difficulty relaxing. It was a relief, however, that at least we had one less child on foreign soil.

After our return from Hawaii, Daniel e-mailed on August 27:

> Hi. We just got back from about 5 days out. We took fire on about 2 occasions and a couple of rockets. I'm sure you heard about the IED that hit our platoon about a week ago and cost one of our guys their leg. He's in the States now and we hope to see him at the [Marine Corps Birthday] Ball in November [the Marine did indeed attend].

> We should be leaving our camp in about a month and won't have to go out after that. We don't always get shot at; it really depends on the luck of the draw. We seem to be getting hit by IEDs a lot more than usual.

He bubbled with comments about the Olympic swimmer from Chico, family news, and all the plans for his return. Quite possibly, his planning for the future was a way to reassure himself that he *was* coming home. If I was increasingly nervous the closer we came to his return date, he must have been more so.

I wrote in an e-mail August 29 to Mario's 2/1 Vietnam veteran friends:

> …This week we are dealing with the third death in our hometown area. This was a Marine KIA, a sergeant.… But there are miracles! The following stories are from the moms in our 2/1 e-mail group during the same week that Daniel went over the IED.
>
> [A] Marine from 2/1 Weapons Company drove over a large IED with both his front *and* rear tires *twice* without it exploding. When the bomb squad got there and took it apart, they said there was a large pressure plate. The bomb had been set perfectly and it was amazing that it hadn't gone off once—much less twice.
>
> Another Marine had, thankfully, dropped off all his guys, and was driving the humvee when he drove over an IED The force blew him out the top of his soft-cover humvee. He didn't pass out nor have a head or spinal cord injury. He looked up to see the humvee about to land on him, and managed to crawl away in time. He had a deep laceration on his leg, which may have cut through the hamstring, giving him a Forrest Gump-type wound near his "but-tocks". He was supposed to go back to his unit (which he wanted to do) and do light duty, but then he got sent home for a 30-day convalescent leave. Maybe they figured that if he was only able to walk with crutches and couldn't sit, he was pretty useless to them and might as well go home. This sounds like the "million dollar wound."

… The latest guestimate is that the battalion will be home on October 8 or 9. One of the moms in our e-mail group said her Marine told her they are starting to cross-train with their replacements. Another lady said her boyfriend was to start classes on base before the rest of the unit returned; he would come early, with the advance party. That news lifted my spirits. It is true; they really *will* be coming home.

As I began to permit myself to think about Daniel coming home, I also became concerned about PTSD. It discouraged me to consider that I might again have to go through the psychological fallout of war. Given the level of constant danger with which the troops in Iraq had to cope—not to mention the violence they had witnessed—it seemed likely there would be difficulty transitioning from warrior to citizen. Many of the support group's sons were about to come home; I thought it might be helpful if we parents had some information about what to expect with homecoming. I began to build a lending library of material about PTSD and developed a reading list. I obtained some information about the services available at the local VA.

I spoke with Mary Tendall, MFT, who is subcontracted to the Veterans Administration to work with veterans experiencing combat-related trauma. I summarized her points to our 2/1 e-mail group:

There will be changes when our Marines come home; they will not be the same. They will probably have some sleep disturbances (e.g., difficulty falling sleep, staying asleep, sleeping too much, or bad dreams) until their nervous systems come out of combat mode, which will take time. They may want to be alone a lot to have time to sort through the many experiences they've had to wall off in order to stay focused while in Iraq. They may need more quiet time for themselves or to connect with their families. They may want few or no social activities at first. This allows them the opportunity to have some control over their environment, which wasn't possible in Iraq.

[Tendall] warned that...these fellows have trouble acknowledging [any problems]; they don't want to feel as if they "can't handle it," and they fear stigma on their military record. [Rather than calling it PTSD] she explains to her vets that staying in combat mode when there is no combat is like an engine that is revved up. The engine needs an adjustment to get back to the right speed for the current situation. She said the vets usually find it easier to accept the concept when she speaks in terms of a nervous system response which needs an adjustment, rather than "stress reaction," PTSD, or anything that hints of personal failing...

I didn't get much response from the e-mail group after I sent that summary, other than a few comments, suggesting their kids seemed to be okay when they called home and that they just needed to get out of combat. In my typical nursing "prepare and prevent" zeal, I probably was too pushy with what I thought the families ought to know and was not sensitive enough to people who weren't ready to think about more negative issues.

Perhaps not every combat veteran develops PTSD, but the situation is ripe for it. Based on my experience, I would like to see a proactive effort: a requirement that all veterans have counseling sessions upon their return. This might reduce the chance of unexamined issues smoldering until the veteran is flooded with nightmares, outbursts of anger, or drug and alcohol problems. Even if the veteran seems to be doing quite well, he or she still could benefit from checking in with a counselor every few months since many symptoms are not apparent for years. Indeed, Mario finds that he has more trouble now with nightmares and irritability than he has had in years. I have learned personally that post-traumatic stress can affect everyone in the family, even the children born after a veteran's time in the military. Sometimes the last person to see the problem is the veteran. For this reason I feel quite passionate about urging—for the sake of the families combat veterans already have or hope to have one day—that returning warriors access counseling, without waiting for symptoms.

By the end of August, I confided in an e-mail to one of the 2/1 moms:

I am very worried about what changes there will be with Daniel as a result of the war. PTSD is *very* real to me.... I don't want to go through that again! I hope that [PTSD] information...may help us deal with things as they come up, rather than after they build up. Maybe PTSD won't become a problem for some, but if I can put information out there that may be helpful to someone else, I'm glad.

I have "been there, done that," but that doesn't mean I necessarily know how to cope with PTSD better than anyone else. In fact, I could benefit from learning something about how to deal with the anger outbursts. I still tend to be paralyzed, like a deer caught in the headlights when someone gets angry—co-worker, another driver, anyone. Not a very useful or therapeutic reaction. But I am determined to do this better now that I have more wisdom and more maturity. If I can help Daniel while keeping my boundaries intact, it will be good for me, but also good for him to learn to respect others' boundaries if he's angry.

All the while, trying to remember that he may do better than I expect and I don't want to start seeing problems where there aren't any.

I spoke with local psychologists, Dr. Jim Park and Dr. Judy Brislain, who have worked with vets and other trauma survivors, and invited them to address those in our local support group who wished to discuss what to expect when our sons came home. As a gesture of appreciation to our military, these professionals graciously donated their after-hours time to speak to us.

The psychologists underscored the need to let the men set their own pace for reuniting with family and friends. Some returning vets welcomed a lot of family at homecoming. Others could cope with only a few, and others didn't want anyone to greet them. Conversely, one of the moms, whose son had returned the week before, related how her son repeatedly said he didn't want anyone to meet him, but was glad when she and her husband showed up anyway.

We were told that one of the things counselors of the 9/11 attack survivors learned was that people needed to tell their stories "a hundred times" in order to help them process the experience. We needed to let these young men talk, if they were willing, and not suggest they "get over it and move on."

While Daniel's tour in Iraq was harrowing, my life would have not been altered as significantly had Daniel returned home at this point. However, I was about to experience by far the most piercing event of Daniel's military service.

Chapter Thirteen

LABOR DAY BOMBING

Mario and I, phones in hand, listened as Daniel described in detail the Labor Day bombing scene. In our darkened bedroom, I was unable to see my husband's expression, but I could sense his anguish. My eyes filled with tears as Daniel's descriptions burned graphic images into my brain.

"Was *anyone* okay?"

"You know, that's the strangest thing. Everyone in the truck was either killed or injured except one Marine. He reached down to get a water bottle from the floor just when it went off. At first we didn't even know who he was, because he was covered in white ash, his gear was blown off, and he seemed stunned. We thought he'd been hurt too and he was taken to be checked out. They told us later that the blast swept over his back, but that nothing happened to him.

"Out of about fifteen guys in the truck, only five weren't killed, but they were pretty f—-up. One Marine was on the ground, moaning constantly; blood was coming from his head, nose, and ears. We also had three Iraqi Special Forces traveling with us. One Iraqi guy's leg was gone and he was screaming so much that it was hard to focus on anything else."

"Mijo, I am so glad you're alive," Mario muttered in a thickened voice.

"Yeah. You know, bad as all that was, do you know the worst part? It was when we picked up what was left of our friends and had to load them onto the trucks. Seeing them piled there, with their arms and legs sticking out at odd angles, that was the worst moment of my life! That picture will stick with me forever."

As he spoke, my brain flashed to photos I had seen of stacks of corpses from concentration camps, jumbled in seemingly careless fashion on flatbed trucks. It hadn't occurred to me before but, of course, the Marines arriving on scene would have to pick up their friends' bodies and clear the area, a dreadful task.

Daniel's voice softened to an anguished whimper, "Mom, those were my friends! If I had been sitting in that first vehicle where I usually sit, I would have been decapitated too. It could have been me. The suicide bomber's car passed right under my nose! Maybe I should have spotted the bomber coming alongside our truck right past me. Maybe I should have been one of the ones killed."

While his own horror was fresh, he gave more explicitly grisly details of the scene (many of which he has asked me not to share), though he seldom speaks of this now. I strained to hear every nuance in his tone of voice. It was most difficult to be so far away when I needed to see the expression in his eyes and I ached to enfold him.

"How are you doing emotionally?" I asked.

"I wouldn't say I was angry—yet."

"How did your commanders handle this?" Mario asked.

"They made us go back to the base for a mandatory meeting with the chaplain. We won't go back out for a few days so that we can decompress. And they're giving us a chance to call home. There aren't enough of us left in the 3rd Platoon who haven't been killed or injured in the last six months, to keep the platoon going. They are disbanding our platoon and we will be split up and reassigned to different platoons."

It seemed to me that Daniel's superiors handled these survivors as sensitively as possible while in a war zone.

"Once the five of us who were not injured or killed were back at the FOB, we just wanted to be together. It was hard to be back at our house and see all the things there that belonged to those guys. A few times we talked about what happened. Mostly we tried to distract ourselves by watching movies, but none of us could concentrate on the stories. We were tired, but no one could sleep."

It seemed as if Daniel spoke for about forty minutes. Over and over we reassured him that we loved him and were so thankful he was alive. Finally the time came to say goodbye. We were so helpless; there wasn't anything we could do for him. It wasn't even possible for us to initiate a phone call over the next few days to find out how he was.

Eleven people were killed that day, four of whom were the suicide bomber and three members of the Iraqi Specialized Forces Battalion, Company B. Five Marines were injured. Seven Marines were killed. One of those killed, Lance Corporal Derek L. Gardner, was from Truck Company, but on that day was attached to Daniel's platoon. The other casualties—four of them Daniel's roommates—were:

Lance Corporal Michael J. Allred
Private First Class David P. Burridge
Lance Corporal Quinn A. Keith
Corporal Joseph C. McCarthy
Corporal Mick R. Bekowsky
Lance Corporal Lamont N. Wilson

We later heard that so many dead and wounded were on the ground the two corpsmen could not manage the scene without help from the other Marines. Daniel has since told us there was very little blood at the scene because the intense heat of the blast had effectively cauterized it. While those who died did so instantly, the quality of battlefield medicine is such that all the injured, despite the severity of their wounds, have survived.

Eerily, Daniel has a photo taken that same morning by someone in the watchtower, just as the convoy headed out of the Forward Operating Base. The camera's eye looks down into the first two trucks. I am able to identify some of the Marines in the first truck as well as Daniel in the second. It is so chilling to see a picture of these young men who are unaware of what will happen to them only a few moments later.

Once Mario and I put our phones in their cradles, there was not a hope we could fall asleep again. We talked a bit about what we'd heard, but were too overwhelmed to say much.

I decided instead to sit at the computer and write a synopsis of our conversation to all those on my "Daniel Update" e-mail list. My hands began to tremble as I typed. By the end of the e-mail my teeth were chattering uncontrollably.

In response to my update e-mail, Mario's 2/1 Vietnam vets encircled us with love and prayers. One of them wrote:

Dear Nanette,

My heart sank as I began reading your news. While Daniel was so very lucky, too many of our other beloved Marines were not. It's impossible to know why such a simple decision to ride in a different vehicle ends up saving your life. It's a decision he will replay over and over through the years. Make sure Mario talks to him about it when he gets home. At some point he will feel guilty that he was spared. He need not, but he will. I am so very happy he was spared, while I mourn the loss of the other good Marines.... May God bless them all and keep them safe.

Semper Fi, Tom Gillespie

Those of us in the Iraq 2/1 e-mail group consoled each other. We shared whatever information we were able to obtain about the suicide bombing. Even though this happened to one small group of Marines in Fox Company, it seemed the entire battalion mourned. To this day, the 2/1 Marines who were in Iraq in 2004—even those who were not in Fox Company—have difficulty speaking of that day.

My grief was somewhat assuaged by action. In the days that followed, I sent hand-written notes to the families for whom I could locate addresses and left online condolences on the Legacy Web site for the others.

My fear for Daniel's emotional well-being sparred with my weak-kneed relief and gratitude to God that my son was alive. I grieved for the mothers whose sons had been killed. I was almost such a mother. All Labor Day morning I had pictured the moment when the casualty officers might come to my door. It took only a small shift to transfer the fear and anguish I had felt to the mothers of those killed. I couldn't even imagine the depth of their anguish, but I felt a strong emotional connection to these women I didn't know.

At home, I was in need of healing too. I felt extraordinarily traumatized by how close Daniel had come. The horror nearly consumed me. For months afterward I experienced intrusive thoughts and vivid images of the bombing scene many times each day. I grieved intensely, as if these events had happened to me.

This response may seem excessive, yet, in my opinion, this is consistent with secondary Post Traumatic Stress Disorder. In 2000, the fourth edition of the psychiatric bible, the *Diagnostic and Statistical Manual of Mental Disorders*, widened its description of PTSD triggers to include "... learning of unexpected or violent death, serious harm, or threat of death or injury experienced by a family member ..." (p. 463)

Further, the understanding of secondary post-traumatic stress has been extended to counselors or therapists who suffer as a result of hearing survivors' vivid accounts of their trauma. Having heard the graphic descriptions of the scene and knowing that my son could easily have been a victim, I believe my reaction fits under both understandings of secondary PTSD.

I'm glad there is awareness now about PTSD. But, while it is right to focus on the effects of war on the warrior, often overlooked is the effect on the family that has loved, suffered, and endured with him both during his combat tour as well as the aftermath of adjustment. Indeed, I feel that families are uniquely vulnerable—more than at any time in history. With instant communication and the availability of live satellite television transmission, families often are witnesses to some of the very same events their warrior has experienced. Families also serve in today's virtual war.

On September 17, Daniel sent us a short e-mail:

> I miss you too, but just remember that this is the most dangerous time of the tour for us. Who knows what is in store for us? We're all nervous and taking no risks at this time. I hope to see you guys in a few weeks, but keep all of

us in your prayers. Love you guys and tell everyone I love
them. Talk to you later … Daniel

It pained me when I read the tentative phrase "hope to see you." The
following day we had another e-mail:

Hi. We just got back from a patrol down a dangerous
route. We all were more worried than we've been for a
while. We made it back together though. Two more of my
friends just died yesterday. One was a guy who I've known
since Chesapeake and another one who everybody in the
company would agree was the best interpreter we had [and]
who had a heart of gold. That makes nine of my friends this
week. Not a good week.

Mike Allred was the hardest death to take. He was
everybody's best friend. Everyone loved him and I never
thought, of all people, he would be gone. He said he was
running out of close calls and needed to hurry up and get
out of here.… Even before he was killed, I told myself that
when I got out I was really going to miss him. We were the
two guys who weren't going to take any leave when we got
back and we were going to lift weights every day.…

It's cooling down now.…

I did get the Under Armour [awhile ago], but I gave it to my
friend who liked it and he was wearing it when he was hit
with the IED that day, so I won't use it now.…

Under Armour was very popular in the first years of the war for its
moisture-wicking properties. The Marine Corps later banned its use when
the men were on patrol. Its synthetic fibers can melt in the intense heat of an
IED blast, causing the fibers to fuse with the skin and intensify the injury.

Doc Worley, one of the two corpsmen who had treated the injured at the Labor Day bombing and who had been reassigned to a different unit after the bombing, suffered a traumatic leg amputation himself in an IED attack that week.

We at home were equally nervous. All the 2/1 families were holding their breaths. On one hand we wanted to encourage positive thinking by focusing on the homecoming; on the other hand, we were superstitious enough to fear that planning for the future would hex it.

The day after the Labor Day bombing, the FRO forwarded the 2/1 families a letter (likely written before the bombing) from the Battalion Commanding Officer, Lt. Col. Gregg Olson:

> We've had about the same challenges we're used to since the last time I sent an update. We're doing the same missions, face the same issues with the weather, the enemy, and the poor people of Iraq who just want to get about their lives in the face of terrorist intimidation. The poor folks caught in the middle…[the ellipse punctuation marks are Olson's] maybe they live next to a family whose sons are terrorists… or maybe the mosque they attend preaches messages of hate rather than the true messages of Islam…they are the ones we are trying hard to win over. We don't even have to make them like us—they just have to recognize who has a vision for the future of Iraq that includes peace and stability…and whose vision includes nothing but repression and violence. Once they figure that out, they may be able to start resisting the terrorists in their own ways. We shall see and time will tell.…

Lt. Col Olson went on to give some information about homecoming. There still was no firm date for the return of the battalion—only a tentative window of possible dates. As a gesture of hope, I made motel reservations near Camp Pendleton for a span of time to cover the entire "window." I felt like a pregnant woman who keeps a bag packed so she can race out the door whenever the big moment arrives.

I hoped Daniel would want to stay with us in the motel when the unit was given their 96-hour liberty upon return, but I tried to allow for the possibility that he might not be ready for so much togetherness. Fortunately, he e-mailed that he definitely wanted us to be there, and he planned to stay with us at the motel.

Shortly after the Labor Day bombing, Mario wrote some personal musings that he intended to give Daniel but never has. I include these because I think they portray well the tumult of a father's emotions when his child is endangered:

> 9/20/04: Dear Daniel, You're almost ready to come home, so it may seem a little strange for me to start a journal [about] my feelings while you're deployed. Honestly, I don't think there would have been a lot of variety of feelings, only their intensity changed from time to time.
>
> The strongest feeling has been fear, fear that you might not come back or come back all f—- up and with a bleak future. This fear has caused me to wake up in the middle of the night in a cold sweat. I know I dream about you because I wake up every morning thinking of you and wondering what you could be doing.
>
> I also want you to know that in spite of my constant fear, I only get stronger in my conviction that your actions are making a difference in the world and especially in this country. I also know the bonds that you're forming with your Marine brothers. That experience alone will make you a better man, husband, father, brother, son, etc.
>
> I never really knew how my father felt. I knew how my mom felt because I let her tell me. My dad probably thought I didn't want to know because I never asked. If he only worried half as much as I have, he worried a lot. I also think everyone felt that the best way to get over it was to

try to forget, and to try to assume a normal life. Except I had had thirteen months to create such high expectations of a "normal" life, nothing even came close. I hope that because you're coming home as a group, the adjustment period won't be so long.

I love you.

9/21/04: Hey, Peanut [Mario's nickname for Daniel]: I know you picked up your e-mail last night. That's comforting to your Mom and me. Even if you don't answer our e-mails, it helps to know you're not in harm's way even if for a moment.

... I'm not sleeping a lot these days; neither is your Mother. I wake up feeling like there's something I should be doing to help ensure your safety. I'd give anything to be at your side. It seems really unfair that it's always the young who have to fix the problems we old people have created for you. Young people always pay for the screw-ups of their previous generation.

Love, Dad

9/23/04: Dear Peanut:... Each day that goes by, I get more excited about seeing you even though I still worry and will not stop until I can hug you. I know you can hardly wait to be home and I hope you're pleased with your welcoming family.

I love you, Dad

[An undated letter] Hi, I heard on the news that we are starting to get aggressive in Fallujah again and worry that things will turn sour again and someone decides to keep you there. I pray it doesn't happen.

... I won't be able to relax until I know you've left that hellhole. I can't count the days because we don't have a date certain for your rotation home. So it's not fun knowing you're "short" [a reference to having a short time left in his tour] and still worry that anything could still change....

I love you, Dad

In late September we began to receive some packages containing his belongings that he had sent ahead of his return. Daniel called to say he had left Camp Baharia (the Marines had nicknamed the camp using words that rhyme with the above name, but that variously describe a common intestinal ailment or a sexually transmitted disease) to a "safer location." It was truly going to be over; I was cautiously relieved.

As excited as I was, I didn't realize how much tension I'd been holding for all our 2/1 sons. The following evening, September 25, Mario and I returned from an early anniversary dinner to find this e-mail from one of the 2/1 parents: "Our [son] just called. Midnight central time. He had just finished his last patrol. At 1300 today [Sunday, the 26th] the 2/1 has no more responsibility in Iraq. He said they were the last to be moved to Camp Fallujah."

A shiver ran up my spine, my eyes welled with tears, and my knees literally felt weak. 2/1 was *done*! It was over! Mario and I had been given the best anniversary present ever. Thank you, God.

Chapter Fourteen

HOMECOMING

As each company from 2/1 completed its final patrol in Iraq, the Marines had to turn in their night scopes and specialized weapons. My relief grew with every little signal that they would not be called back to duty. Our sons had been waiting for several days for a convoy to take them to an airfield. On October 4 Daniel e-mailed us they were at Taquadum, a town with a much safer airstrip than Baghdad Airport's. Daniel e-mailed, "We should be good from here on out.... See you soon."

He phoned Damián while he was awaiting transport to Kuwait. They chatted superficially about items in the news (Scott Peterson's trial and Paris Hilton's lost dog, to name two). Daniel said he wasn't sorry he had joined the Marine Corps, but he did have negative feelings at least about the "bad guys" who lived in Fallujah. He also mentioned he planned to drink a lot of beer when he was finally able to buy some.

Mario was giddy with relief. In another unsent missive:

> 9/28/04: Hi, Mijo, I hadn't realized how miserable I felt until I heard you were not going out any more. I've even been able to laugh and have a good time with other people. Before, I just wanted people to leave me alone. Even when I knew they were concerned, I thought they were negative about the situation.

... I'm getting more and more excited about your homecoming. I wished I knew with certainty when that will be so I can actually count the days....

Love, Dad

In the Web guest book for the Vietnam veterans of 2/1, Mario wrote (ironically on the day 2/1 would end operations in Iraq):

"Though he should conquer a thousand men in the battlefield, yet he, indeed, who would conquer himself is the noblest victor."

I recently read this in a Buddhist book and it hit me with the realization my son will have to fight those demons we all know so well. You all did something to show support for our troops: care packages, letters, e-mail, prayers, etc. I think our real work is still ahead of us, and that is to make sure that the day after the parade streamers are swept away, we help our troops deal with the remnants of war that remain in the depths of our nightmares. I know we will answer this call, also, and find solace in the satisfaction that comes with helping our Brothers.

As my son Daniel gets "short" and cheats death day-to-day, my fears grow, along with the anticipation of his homecoming. I go from elation to fright faster than the speed of light. I also fear the battles within him to come. I can only hope that I can be a catalyst to him and help him cope with his feelings. I know there is no cure, only acceptance and learning to control his reactions. If not, I know he has all of you to call on.

I will never stop counting my blessings to have you as my
Marine family and to know that I am not alone.

THANK YOU,

OOOO-RAH, Semper Fi, Mario

About this time, Mario's 2/1 veteran friend, "Stormy" (Tom Matteo),
sent Daniel a welcome-home e-mail that even now, years later, touches me. I
think it is such a wise mixture of pride, love, and understanding that I wish
to share it (I have corrected typographical errors and punctuation for the
sake of clarity, but not altered the content of the letter):

October 4, 2004

Dear Daniel,

I wanted to take this opportunity to write this letter to you,
since I will not be able to attend your homecoming this
week in California.

I cannot express to you the gratitude and sincere appreciation
that I have for you and your fellow Marines, who have given
so much for America over the last year's combat action.

I had told you, before you left, that combat will change
Human Beings and that you need to address the issues of
war soon after you return home. The day is here and I want
you to know that you have the support of your family and
your country behind you. Your emotions will run high for
a period of time and then you will find yourself lost.

You will try [to] find a solution to the war and you will
question yourself in asking, "Did I do the right things each
day as a Marine?" You are alive by God's choice and any

day or night you could have been a KIA. You did the right things and your training and will to live kept you safe from all those close calls.

The excitement will finally cease in a few weeks and your emotions will change without your knowing it. That's when you need to sit down with Dad and have a long talk. He will not have all the answers but, rest assured, he knows what he will be talking about.

Remember the 'hoorah' and reality of war will finally settle in and you will realize all that you have been through with your fellow Marines. Do not forget a one of them, both alive and dead. Each one of the men and women that you had the honor to serve with in combat is a hero and you are in that same group, my friend. So always honor your service each day of your life.

Keep these men and women close to your heart and understand that they died doing what they loved best: being a United States Marine. They [did] no different[ly] than what you would have done for the Corps and your Country. You are forever changed and now have the honor of being one of the men who have given so much for freedom and liberty for all mankind. You are 'Daniel, A Combat Marine', something that nobody can ever take from you!

Take care,

Love, Stormy, S/SGT USMC

Everyone in Daniel's battalion had to stay in Kuwait for several days of decompressing on the base there, where they were given some mandatory end-of-deployment group counseling. Daniel says it mostly consisted of rather superficial advice, such as "Don't beat your wife when you get home."

The time frame for return was fluid. The Marines were using chartered commercial airplanes. Initially Fox Company was to have returned in the afternoon of the very first day of homecoming. The days and times ended up changing at least five more times—one change came only a day before we were supposed to have left for Camp Pendleton. Semper Gumby.

In the end, Fox and Echo Companies, rather than being in the first wave of returnees, were now scheduled to be in the very last—arriving in the wee hours of Friday, October 9. I was disappointed; the change in the schedule also meant that I would not meet some of the parents in our e-mail group whose Marines were arriving days earlier. We were fortunate to live only a ten-hour drive away; I felt sorry for those who would have to make—and revise—airline reservations.

While we were driving to the homecoming, Daniel called us in high spirits from the airport in Baltimore. His plane had landed for refueling and he and many other Marines had headed straight to the bars for their own refueling. Daniel was on U.S. soil at last.

Our little troupe arrived on base close to midnight to await the 3:00 AM arrival of Fox Company. While we waited, we met some of the Fox Company parents with whom we'd corresponded all these months. I also had made several "Welcome Home!" posters for Daniel as well as for some of the Marines whose parents were unable to attend; I hoped to give them an unofficial *in loco parentis* welcome-home hug.

The homecoming ritual called for the Marines to arrive at March Air Force Base and then be taken by bus for the approximately ninety-mile drive to Camp Pendleton. Several Marines who had been wounded during the deployment and had been recuperating stateside had also come to greet their buddies. The returning Marines were thrilled to see their friends.

Upon the Marines' arrival at Camp Pendleton's battalion headquarters area at Camp Horno, the first order of business was to return to the battalion armory all the weapons that had been taken to Iraq. Once that was accomplished, the Marines got into formation by companies before marching onto the field, some walking with the aid of crutches. Wearing only their desert camouflage utilities and floppy boonie hats, the Marines must have found the drizzly, dense fog of the pre-dawn morning quite chilly after the heat of Iraq.

A minute's worth of formal words was spoken to the troops by one of the officers. Then each platoon was dismissed. At 3 o'clock on a Saturday morning, only serious welcomers were present. With no more than about three hundred Marines and their families on the parade deck, it was not difficult to locate Daniel.

Oddly, I could not cry. I am not sure whether I was being elaborately careful to give Daniel emotional space, whether I sensed Daniel might be displeased by an overly sentimental response, or whether my emotions were blunted. Nonetheless, I was glad to have him in my arms, to actually be able to touch him after all these months.

Once everyone had his or her Marine, no one stood around to socialize. We gathered Daniel's gear and headed for the motel for a few hours' sleep. On the way, we dropped off one of the 3rd Platoon's corpsmen. Daniel proudly introduced him as "Doc Santos, the best Corpsman in the entire Marine Corps!"

An e-mail I sent on October 13 to Daniel's former counselor here at home summarized those few days with Daniel:

> Got back last night [from Camp Pendleton]. It was hard to leave Daniel after I'd just gotten him back. But I'll see him this weekend since he will fly to the Bay Area to visit Mario's family, who want to have a small gathering of family and friends for him. He said that was okay. He wasn't quite ready to come to Chico yet. Daniel didn't take leave [he only used the 96-hour liberty given to every Marine when he spent time with us at homecoming] because he wanted to save leave for the holidays. He'll take advantage of some weekends and Thanksgiving to see us. He is talking about wanting to go to [junior] college next fall and take classes possibly with the intent to get himself on track to go to CSU and eventually become a teacher (amazing, school never interested him before). He is eager to get on with the next non-Marine phase of his life....

When the plane [carrying the Marines from Kuwait] crossed into American airspace, the pilot dipped the wings and the guys went nuts, knowing they were in our skies.

… I am relieved, but still my heart is inexplicably heavy. I'm not sure if it's just grief for what they had to go through, grief for what we went through, my own survivor guilt, or just the inability to emotionally switch gears so fast. Heck, as much as I was too wound up with all the [events of the] past several months, I too will suffer a little withdrawal from all the constant adrenalin.

… We watched some movies on DVD in the motel room. But that's all he seemed to feel like doing. Went on the base, so he could buy the seven medals and ribbons he knew he had earned before they sold out (have to be ready to put them on the front of his dress blues for the Marine Corps Birthday Ball on November 10). Mario and I got more Marine pins and T-shirts to add to our already-vast collection. Daniel wanted to go shopping at the mall in Oceanside. He seemed to be okay—even in the mall crowds, which have apparently been difficult for some returnees. But I would guess most tend to be okay the first few days. Mario and I found we would wake up in the night and look over at him sleeping on the other bed, just to make sure he was really there. He did develop 4 rolls of film—only one of which he would show us. But that one roll had pictures of the house they lived in, the highway signs in Arabic, and the seven memorial crosses with photos of each of the guys killed in the suicide bombing.

Daniel wasn't yet ready to drive the car on the freeway. While sitting in the back seat on the driver's side, he admitted to being nervous when cars pulled up to pass us on the highway. Other than that, he seemed "normal."

The first day we were together he talked a bit about his experiences but, after that, the window of opportunity faded, and he didn't speak much more about them.

I tried hard to remind myself to let him tell me what he wanted to, but his experiences lay heavily between us. I guess what I wanted was for him to respond as women like to: to "go over" everything. I wanted to hear all about whatever it was that he went through. If he had to experience it, I wanted to hear all about it. And I wanted to share our experience with him: how frightened we were for him and how much we loved him. But I could see that he didn't want to speak of his experiences or to hear about ours. Whatever made me think he would want to dissect it all? That was *my* need, not his. When I started to say something heartfelt to Daniel, he just whined that I was corny. I felt rather discarded after that comment. I know there are surely many perfectly understandable reasons for Daniel's reticence. Quite possibly he couldn't handle any more pain including—or perhaps, especially—ours.

I see now that we had the unreasonable expectation that after all our pain, it was our turn to share. I confess that I hoped to find mutual comfort in exchanging stories, but in retrospect, that was an inappropriate expectation. Still, it was hard to accept that it might be a decade before Daniel might ever want to hear how it had been for us. Or it might be never.

Mario and I entered a period when we felt grieved and aggrieved. Our own sorrow was a heavy weight. Our hearts felt bruised, our feelings easily hurt.

During his homecoming weekend we asked Daniel if it was okay if we had a welcome-home party for him sometime in the next four or six weeks. He demurred; he did not want a party. I accepted that calmly until Mario's sister-in-law called that same weekend to talk to Daniel. After welcoming him home, she told Daniel she wanted to give him a party. I felt so rejected when he agreed to their party for the following weekend in the Bay Area.

Once again, Mario and I were jealous. If anyone were to give Daniel a party, why shouldn't it be us? Daniel may well have felt that he didn't know how to say "no" gracefully to Mario's family, and may have felt that politeness dictated that he assent. We understood all that, but it didn't keep us from feeling disregarded and hurt. After all, *we* were the parents. *We* had sweat blood for Daniel. *We* spent sleepless nights worrying about him. *We* suffered. And, once more—as was the case for his twenty-first birthday—*they* got to give the party, as if *they* were the parents.

Peevishly, Mario and I began to fear that Daniel preferred his uncle's family to ours. I was ashamed of my mean-spirited emotions. If I could have controlled which emotions came to me, I would not have wanted to feel this way. The months that followed Daniel's return were turning out to be as much an emotional minefield, in their own way, as the deployment had been.

Mario's brother had once told me he loved Daniel like one of his sons— he worried as much as a parent might while Daniel had been deployed. While I can't know exactly how it was for him, I feel certain that no one can fully appreciate a parent's experience till one lives it. A case in point: Despite witnessing what the parents in our support group went through and identifying closely with them, I still was not able to fully comprehend the intensity of the deployment experience, with its roller-coaster emotions and 24/7 anxiety, until it happened to me.

In fairness, I was well aware that it had never occurred to Mario's family that we might feel that they were pre-empting us with regard to the twenty-first birthday party or the homecoming party. They had no desire to take over; they were merely trying to do something nice for our son, whom they truly loved. For that reason I found my reaction all the more shameful and upsetting.

I find it embarrassing to describe these unattractive emotions. Mario and I were having a rather flamboyant pity party. We knew Daniel might have some post-deployment adjustment issues; we didn't expect that we would too. I suspect other families whose children have returned home from combat have experienced similar feelings or others just as confusing and upsetting.

An obvious way of handling this would have been to tell Mario's family how we felt. Though we knew our feelings weren't reasonable, we were unable to trust ourselves to not say something intemperate. Till we could achieve some emotional distance, it seemed wiser not to broach the topic. I wasn't sure how to handle the morass of my feelings. I didn't like them, but they were there anyway. It seemed that the only thing I could do was to silently acknowledge that I had these feelings, but not permit myself to act on them.

Feeling put on the shelf by Daniel and feeling as if Mario's brother had replaced us, we didn't feel like going to the party. However, after seven months of not seeing Daniel, we didn't want to pass up an opportunity to see him now that he was home. Daniel had just barely escaped death; what was wrong with us that we now were aggravated with him?

I think Mario and I felt Daniel "owed" us more time and bonding than he may have wanted—or been able at that time—to give. Besides, other people wanted and deserved his time and attention too. If Mario and I didn't go to the party we would only have hurt ourselves.

Daniel had elected to save some of his leave for the Christmas holidays and to use the rest of it to exit the Marine Corps a little earlier than his scheduled discharge date of June 2005. Most of his battalion took their month-long post-deployment leave right after homecoming and went to visit their families. All were to be back in time for the Marine Corps Birthday Ball in November. Those Marines, like Daniel, who were not on leave remained on base performing odd jobs until everyone in the unit had returned.

Daniel's homecoming party happened just one month before the 2004 presidential election. As we drove to the Bay Area, political slogans covered billboards and car bumpers. The entire nation seemed polarized. Politics was a fiery topic at any gathering. Feelings were intense and passionate; people from both parties seemed to like one candidate but loathe the other. Though I looked at the rhetoric and positions of both candidates regarding world and national events, I found that, for me, the tie-breaker was which candidate I wanted for my son's Commander-in-Chief.

Mario despised one of the presidential candidates for reasons that went back to that person's disposition in the Vietnam War. Especially when political outcomes affected the safety of our military or if a discussion touched on Vietnam and those who served there, Mario took political discussion very personally. Some family members supported the candidate Mario despised, which he interpreted as repudiation of him and of his experience as a Vietnam vet. Mario, the consummate icon of family ties and loyalty, found that, since Daniel had been in Iraq, there were some family members he no longer wished to be with and had begun to avoid.

I realize I am being evasive about our political preferences, but my point—to highlight some of the emotional issues that ambushed Mario and me—is apolitical.

When we pulled into his brother's driveway, Mario was particularly affronted to see several large campaign posters for the "other" candidate on the front lawn (apparently placed there not by Mario's brother but by another family member—deliberately, we were told—to annoy Mario, as a "joke"). Instead, Mario felt as if he'd been slapped; he wanted to turn around right then and drive home.

Of course, this was Mario's brother's home; his brother had a perfect right to allow any sign on the lawn that he wished. We were way too thin-skinned. We knew this was thumb-sucking self-pity at its most ugly, but the feelings were there nonetheless. Others expected us to be okay now that Daniel was uninjured and had come home—and I think we subconsciously expected the same. But we were still on the emotional roller coaster of the last four years and overwrought from the acute stress of the previous seven months. We still grieved for Daniel's experience, for our experience, and for the experience of the families of the dead Marines. The bombing had changed my life; I was still trying to regain my equilibrium.

The effort to override our emotions and try to act rationally was stressful, but had to be done. During the last few years, we wanted to cross off certain family members (on my side as well as his), yet we knew that, when all was said and done, people were more important than politics. And these people were inherently good-hearted. They also loved us. We could not allow ourselves to give in to our emotions.

We went into the house, spoke with Daniel, and visited with Mario's family and their friends. Daniel commented later that some of the partygoers felt the need to tell him that our country shouldn't be in Iraq, that the war was wrong. Some young adults piously reminded him that war is bad; peace is good. Daniel managed to let it go, but it angered him.

Such conversation-stoppers actually occurred fairly frequently. We had friends who e-mailed us to say they were glad to know Daniel was home safe from Iraq, but "we have reservations about the war." I don't know why everyone felt obliged to qualify the good wishes. Couldn't someone merely be glad for us without having to qualify it? I longed for someone to ask about Daniel without adding "but…"

There were strangers who, totally unbidden and a propos of nothing, approached Daniel, knowing he was an Iraq veteran, and unloaded their negative opinions of the war or the President's policies. Such actions are insensitive, at best, and ill-mannered, at worst.

Why acquaintances—and especially strangers—feel the need to criticize the mission to the same person that risked his life and lost friends for that mission is puzzling. Many of the military families we know report that they seem to have become the target for opinions, frustrations and criticisms of others. Our military did not make the policy that people complain to them about. Undoubtedly some military persons don't care for the policy themselves. Yet they have promised to obey the orders of the Commander-in-Chief and their military superiors, whether they personally agree or not.

I used to feel that it was possible for persons to support the troops even while not supporting the war effort—until my son was in the war. Then it began to feel schizophrenic when people avowed their support of the troops while being vehemently opposed to their mission. I know that I could only deal with supporting and loving Daniel while he was in Iraq.

When those at Daniel's homecoming party who were opposed to the war in Iraq told my son, "Thank you for your service" (an awkward phrase, to be sure), what did they mean? Along the lines of: "Thank you for your service—in the war we think you shouldn't have been in, the war that is immoral?" The last comments cancel out the goodwill of the first—at least for me.

Mario used the following analogy: telling a soldier or Marine that you support them but cannot support what they do is much like telling a middle-aged man with a newborn, "Congratulations. Your baby is cute. I am really happy for you. But I can't believe you did that! What a mistake! What the hell were you thinking when you made a baby at your age?" The tenor of the times suggests that the populace likewise is having a harder time separating the war from the warrior.

As happened at many social gatherings after the Iraq war started, members of Mario's family began to discuss politics at Daniel's welcome-home party. Inevitably, tempers flared; some took umbrage at another's contrary views or ridiculed the other for having such views.

My maternal extended family, as well, has a long history of engaging in political debate whenever they assemble. A veneer of civility may allow relationships to remain intact. The politics themselves are less of an issue; it's the negativity engendered by political issues that I find abhorrent.

Family members and friends have said very hurtful things. The negative comments, however, were sometimes more personal: deriding my son for his "stupidity" in joining the military at all, or accusing him and us of being "brainwashed." It has been emotionally arduous to maintain the connections with family and friends under these conditions. Even now, years later, we still feel uncomfortable with some people.

At the end of the San Francisco weekend, Daniel flew back to Camp Pendleton, but he returned to San Francisco the following weekend. Daniel's Tio Luis's Air Force Academy soccer team was playing a nearby Bay Area college team. It was the first opportunity since his return from Iraq for Daniel to see his uncle and his cousin Marcus (who was still playing on the USAFA soccer team).

I knew that Daniel hadn't seen his Air Force Academy cousin for a long time and two other same-age cousins lived in the Bay Area. I also understood that, having been gone from Chico for as many years as he had, Daniel had few friends any more in his hometown. Nonetheless, try as I might, that poisonous feeling of jealousy once more seeped into my veins. Daniel visited his uncle's house twice, but had yet to come to Chico. We felt like chopped liver. After we suggested that he visit at Thanksgiving, Daniel started to back away from that too. Mario and I were hurt.

Only recently was Daniel able to express how difficult he found it to finally come home. His experiences in Iraq had changed him. He was no longer innocent; he couldn't be our little boy again. I think he was afraid that he might let us down and needed more time to get comfortable with how he had changed.

During the weeks spent waiting for the rest of the Marines to return from their post-deployment leaves, Daniel was tasked with guarding the Armory at Camp Pendleton. Each battalion has its own armory, so the pool of guards for 2/1's armory necessarily came from those who had just returned from Iraq. Guard duty is a solitary job. Daniel found it depressing to be alone with his thoughts—particularly being so recently returned from combat—for entire shifts. Considering those for whom the recent combat experiences were becoming their personal demons, I wondered if there was a greater risk of suicide associated with solitary guard duty shifts? Once the thrill of homecoming has passed, are the newly-returned Marines more vulnerable?

I called Daniel frequently in these weeks to try to keep his spirits up as well as to gauge his emotional status. Though it sounded as though his mood was low when he was on guard duty at the armory, overall he seemed to be psychologically sturdy. Nonetheless, he wasted no time in trying to obtain a different duty, and within several weeks had transferred out of the armory.

Because there are so many Marines at Camp Pendleton, each unit headquartered there holds its own ball throughout the weeks surrounding the Corps' birthday. All the Marines in 2/1 were required to complete their personal leaves prior to their ball. Daniel's dress blues were cleaned, tailored, pressed, the medals jangling from the breast. Daniel said he was looking forward to the ball since it would be the last time that all the Marines would be together as 2/1. Some would be "separating" from active duty in the Corps, transferred, and/or promoted to other battalions. Daniel reported that he enjoyed the ball.

Since Daniel would be separating from the Marine Corps in June, he would not be training with 2/1 for their next Iraq deployment in the summer of 2005. In order to make room for those Marines who would be transferring into 2/1 for the next training cycle, Daniel was required to leave the battalion barracks after Christmas. He and his combat buddies stayed together in the barracks as long as possible; there was comfort in each other's company. It wasn't long before some of these same Marines completed their active-duty commitment and exited the Marine Corps. One of Daniel's friends—the one who had been with him in FAST Company and again in Fox Company, 3rd Platoon—exited the Marine Corps that winter and went home to Texas. Of those remaining few from 3rd Platoon, all were due to exit over the course of the next eight months. This remnant, remaining at the base, bonded more tightly still.

During mid-November of 2004, Marines from other battalions that were deployed in Iraq, as well as brigades from the Army, made a joint assault on Fallujah to eradicate the insurgents there. One of the moms in our hometown group had a Marine son who was involved in the assault. Although I was glad Daniel was not there, I found myself reacting just as if he were: waking up in the night, worrying, and being unable to fall asleep again until I had said a prayer for the Marines. I tried to keep myself from panicking when I heard any bad news. I had yet to master creating enough distance between world events and myself. I learned that it isn't always over when it's over.

As Veterans' Day approached, I wanted to write each of the families who had lost a son in the car bombing. With their grief so fresh, I thought the Veteran's Day might be particularly difficult for them. I struggled with myself because I wanted to be sure that my motivation wasn't mere over-identification with these mothers. I decided to write each of the families a handwritten note. I really wanted the notes to arrive before the holiday, but since composing messages unique to each family took more time than I expected, regrettably some notes arrived late. Weeks later, I received a letter from one mother. I cringed when I read that she hadn't gotten my card till the day after the holiday and was dumfounded when I read that my note had arrived on her son's birthday, the day after Veteran's Day. She was so pleased that someone remembered him on his birthday. Amazing. My tardiness was, in fact, perfect timing.

Mario and I were still quite mopey about Daniel not coming home. One of the moms in the 2/1 e-mail group wrote me. She listed some of the similarities between Daniel's combat stress reaction and her son's. She lent me some perspective about this. I was a bit defensive when a support group friend gently scolded that this wasn't about me, though I reluctantly had to agree that she was right. In spite of the fact that Mario and I had been anguished for so long, we had to put our neediness aside and put our child's needs ahead of ours. And truly his needs were more important.

I think Mario and I deluded ourselves that, if we knew ahead of time about the possible reactions to homecoming, we could avoid them. If we were having this much trouble recovering—and we hadn't even been in Iraq—how much more patient we needed to be in allowing Daniel to adjust in whatever way he needed to.

As soon as we emotionally acquiesced to Daniel's need, Daniel did decide to come home for a few days at Thanksgiving. He'd been given a ninety-six-hour liberty, so he didn't have to take vacation days out of his personal leave accumulation, saving them instead for use at the end of his four-year commitment.

Mirabile dictu! All our children, as well as my mother, were actually at our house for Thanksgiving. I found myself more relaxed about Daniel's psychological health after I'd seen him for a few days. In general, he seemed to be doing well. He found loud noises and barbeque odors brought troublesome memories; but for the most part, he was doing well. He and those members of the 3rd Platoon still in the Marine Corps seemed to be close, spending a lot of time with each other when on base, and calling each other on cell phones, even during the holiday.

By December my grief was easing a bit. I permitted myself to enjoy things a bit more and with less guilt, though, as always, sadness would surface with the slightest of visual or auditory triggers. One weekend in December Mario and I traveled to see our son Damián, who had a role in his college's production of *Amahl and the Night Visitors*. The Menotti operetta, which had been televised every Christmas when I was a child, was one that I remembered and loved. The last scene I have always found poignant, in which the mother sings a tender goodbye aria to her young son, whom she knows she may never see again. This year I found myself sobbing for Amahl's mother and, before I knew it, my sobbing had mutated to sobbing for myself—that other mother who just a few months before had said goodbye to her son at the airport, fearing that he might not ever come back to her. It was as if I was above looking down upon myself and seeing the mother I had been in February and feeling again her anguish. In a dissociated way, I cried for and with that other mother that was myself, at the same time as I cried for the mother in the play.

Daniel again came to Chico just before Christmas and agreed to let us have a small gathering celebrating his homecoming. To help take the spotlight off him we combined this with a welcome-home celebration for his sister, who was home on a break between semesters at the University of Hawaii. About twenty of our close friends and those of our children were invited. Daniel specifically wanted us to invite our local military family support group. He thought the people in our group were "pretty cool." It ended up being a delightful and festive gathering with some of my wonderful and supportive friends in attendance. Daniel and Clarissa enjoyed each other's friends as well. I think Daniel felt at home with our guests and he knew none would challenge his service or preach to him. He even spoke frankly about some aspects of the Labor Day bombing to some of the guests from our support group. I interpreted his candor as a healthy sign. The son of one family in our local support group, also a Marine in 2/1 who had deployed to Fallujah with Daniel, joined us for our gathering as well. I am glad we could honor his homecoming too.

One day I was surfing the web and stumbled onto a Web site that offered memorial bracelets. For those of us who were around during the Vietnam War, the bracelets are an expansion on the concept we remember as the "POW bracelet." I ended up ordering a customized bracelet for myself to honor the Marines killed that day. I realized that for months I had been keeping these young men in the front of my mind, subconsciously fearing that if I didn't, I was somehow dishonoring their memory. By wearing the bracelet, I discovered a sense of relief and comfort to know that I honored these men even in the moments I was not consciously thinking of them. I wore the bracelet daily for years, only removing it after the fifth anniversary of their deaths. I still have the bracelet; it has been an important part of my healing.

Christmas 2004 was spent with Mario's family. And, though we hadn't looked forward to going to the Bay Area again because of the awkwardness of our emotions, it really ended up being a good Christmas after all. Oddly, all four years that Daniel was in the Marine Corps, he was able to be with us for each Christmas.

Chapter Fifteen

WINDING DOWN

In January of 2005, CNN's program, *Paula Zahn Now*, aired a segment about Daniel's platoon. The title of the segment was the platoon's radio call sign, *Pale Rider 3*. The interview focused on the events during the entire seven months of the Fallujah deployment. Featured in the interview were the parents of one of the Marines killed in the Labor Day suicide bombing as well as several remarkable survivors from that day: the platoon's lieutenant, the sergeant who led the squad, and the Navy corpsman who later suffered the traumatic amputation. I found the trio to be inspirational, and I learned a lot about the cohesiveness of Daniel's platoon. Towards the end of the segment, there was a photo of Marines standing at attention during the memorial service held at the Forward Operating Base. In the forefront of the photo I spotted Daniel; I could even decipher his last name on his utilities. I cried when I watched the program, but I appreciated that it allowed me to meet some of the exceptional people who had served with Daniel. I was so impressed with their caliber. In the end, despite the segment being sad for me, it also was healing. Daniel thought the program was "pretty good" too.

In the last few months, before the end of his time in the Marine Corps, Daniel seemed to settle into an easy routine. He went to classes on base that were designed to help acquaint Marines with military benefits after discharge and to help them find employment and/or go to college. He also was promoted to the rank of corporal and was full of plans for his "afterlife." I was relieved when, in fact, he chose to move back to Chico.

Daniel went online to scout for future apartment possibilities and lined up one of his cousins to share the living arrangements. He used the Internet to search for used cars in Chico. He investigated class listings and registration procedures at the local junior college. He arranged to assist his uncle with his two-week soccer camp at the Air Force Academy in the early summer. He was looking with excitement towards his new future.

I know that during that time Daniel was aware, and annoyed, that I was monitoring him with a clinical eye. However, the Vietnam years with Mario taught me well that PTSD, Combat Fatigue, Combat Stress Reaction—call it what you will—can be delayed till long after the original trauma. So far, I didn't note any evidence of emotional difficulty.

In March of 2005, though Mario had to work, I took some vacation days during the University's break. During my week off, I had lots of time for solitude, and I found time to reflect and to write. It was as if, only when looking back as if I were a stranger watching myself, could I honor what I had endured.

In April of 2005, I became aware of a program, Operation Homecoming, sponsored by the National Endowment for the Arts. The NEA issued an open call for essays, stories, poems, journal entries, memoirs, original letters, or other literary forms from military persons or their immediate families describing their experiences since September 11, 2001. A panel that included writers and veterans read all of the submissions. The Library of Congress has agreed to archive all contributions. Some submissions, selected by the panel, were to be considered for inclusion in an anthology scheduled for publication the following year. Andrew Carroll, editor of several best-selling books of war letters—some of which have become subjects of PBS documentaries—had agreed to edit the anthology *pro bono* after the panel had chosen the selections.

Over a period of three or four days, I honed my essay into eight pages and mailed it off. It was eight months before I got word that it was initially selected to be included in the anthology published by Random House. However, because of the publisher's space limitations my piece was eventually cut,

though the NEA included an edited version in their Operation Homecoming
Web site.

Now that Daniel would be leaving active duty, I felt it made sense to
turn the Military Family Support Group over to someone whose loved one
was still in the military. Accordingly, in April, Chris, a mother who had
been a charter member of our group and whose two children were both
Marines, agreed to take the gavel from me. The support group gave Mario
and me a wonderful surprise thank-you party and an album with photos
of their military child as well as wonderful comments. In addition to the
current members of the support group, members from the beginning years
of the group, whose sons had already completed their military service, also
attended. We were honored by the kindness that all the members showed
us. As it had been for the previous four years, we felt uplifted by the group's
support and love.

Chapter Sixteen

ADJUSTING TO CIVILIAN LIFE

In May Daniel came home for good. His apartment lease didn't start till August, when his cousin planned to move to Chico. For the first five weeks after his discharge, Daniel stayed with us, in his old room.

It allowed me the chance to see Daniel over time. Overall, I was reassured. He admitted he knew he had PTSD, though he didn't want to explain to me just what symptoms he had. He was determined to document his PTSD and his hearing loss with the Veterans Administration. While Daniel's hearing loss at certain decibel levels began during the live-fire training exercises years before, it definitely worsened after he drove over the IED.

During June, Daniel drove to Colorado with his Bay Area cousins to visit his uncle and their other cousins. On the way, he dropped his cousins off for a day at a friend's house, and drove a hundred miles to meet for the first time the family of his Marine friend killed in the Labor Day bombing. I was impressed; I don't think I could have done that when I was twenty-two.

Daniel decided to travel to Guatemala later in the summer, staying for three weeks to see family and be carefree. His Bay Area cousins joined him there for part of the time. Mario and I shook our heads, thinking that he ought to be more frugal, that a trip would sap his financial resources. We were wrong; I think it ended up a very good thing for him. It placed him with people totally dissociated from Iraq. Daniel was well distracted by the total change of scenery, language, and customs. It seemed to refresh him.

At the end of August he registered as a part-time student at the local junior college, while working part-time. His apartment was about two miles from our house, but he lived there for only a few weeks. For reasons that had nothing to do with Daniel, his cousin's situation changed and Daniel needed to live with us until the following January, when he planned to travel again to Guatemala for several months in order to attend a Spanish language school. He explained he knew that he would have to settle down when he returned to California, but that he really wanted this time to be carefree. I understood it, but was nervous he might decide to live in Guatemala and we would see him only occasionally from now on. Daniel offered reassurance, saying he would be back on the first of May, at which point he would apply himself steadfastly to get through college. He was true to his word.

In the fall of 2005, Mario's Marine Vietnam Veterans of 2/1 held their annual reunion in Reno. Board members of the veterans' organization decided to present a plaque to the current 2/1 Marines recognizing their actions on the battlefield as "upholding the highest traditions" of 2/1 and of the Marine Corps. The planners for the reunion hoped that some of the current 2/1 Marines would come. As a gesture of respect among brothers, the reunion group wanted these Marines to be their guests. There was a small problem: in late summer 2005, 2/1 was once more in Iraq. The only 2/1 Iraq Marines who were available to attend the reunion were those who, like Daniel, were no longer in the Marine Corps. We were able to contact a few of those former Marines, but Daniel and Darrell Carter, the son of Phyllis from my 2/1 e-mail group, were the only ones in a position to attend. Darrell had moved to Northern California, and a trip to Reno was within relatively easy distance. As representatives for the deployed Marines, these two Iraq vets accepted the plaque from the Vietnam Veterans of 2/1. (When 2/1 returned in February, Mario, as a representative of the Vietnam Veterans of 2nd Battalion, 1st Marines, planned to attend the homecoming and re-present the plaque to the battalion to display in the headquarters' trophy case.)

After the bad experiences Vietnam vets endured from the public through the years—and, indeed, sometimes from vets of earlier wars—these Vietnam vets went to enormous effort to make sure they treated their little brothers with much kindness and generosity. Neither Darrell nor Daniel wanted for anything during their stay in Reno. Their drinks, meals, and rooms were paid by several of the Vietnam veterans— touching gestures from persons who had not received similar symbols of respect and gratitude for their service. The older vets wanted to hear of the experiences of their younger counterparts and the Iraq vets, in turn, seemed to enjoy hearing the Vietnam vets' stories.

The last event of the reunion was a banquet and a fundraising oral auction. One of the items for auction was a Marine Corps lap blanket with the Eagle, Globe, and Anchor insignia on it. Darrell kept bidding on it, even when the bidding began to get outrageously high. The bidding finally got too high for Darrell and he had to drop out. When one of the Vietnam Marines finally won the bidding war for the blanket—four times its true value— he promptly presented it to Darrell.

As happens every year, my husband had difficulty leaving his Marine brothers at the conclusion of the reunion. Memories had been relived, new ones were made, and restorative friendships re-kindled.

Just before Thanksgiving, as I still did daily, I checked the press releases from the Department of Defense listing those who had been killed in Iraq or Afghanistan. That was how I learned that eight Marines from 2/1 were killed in an ambush during Operation Steel Curtain in Iraq. Four of the eight were people Daniel knew from his Iraq deployment. I didn't know any of the eight; but we were a 2/1 family and these were *our* men. The depth of my sadness caused me to realize that, even a year later, my wounds hadn't healed.

After Christmas, Daniel began storing his belongings, preparatory to his going to Guatemala for four months. It was hard to watch him begin to pack.

"I know it's bothering you that I'm going, but I promise I'll come back in a few months. I'm a little sad packing too. It's kind of like packing for Iraq again."

Exactly.

In the end, this trip was very therapeutic for him and it allowed us to detach from him in a healthier way.

Soon enough, Mario and I were focused on milestone events. January was flying by. Our first grandchild Jacinta Maria—courtesy of Damián and Katie—was born on the last day of the month. It was only a few weeks after that event that I retired from the Student Health Center, having worked there for twenty-eight years.

Chapter Seventeen

HEALING THE FATHER THROUGH THE SON

The day after I retired, Mario and I traveled to Camp Pendleton. The Navy ships carrying Daniel's former unit, 2/1, were due to arrive on Saturday, February 18, from their tour in Iraq. Mario had communicated with some of the officers for the battalion to coordinate the presentation of the plaque to the returning Marines.

Mario had issued an open invitation on his organization's Web site to any of the 2/1 Marine Vietnam veterans to attend the homecoming and assist him with the plaque presentation. Two of the Vietnam veterans showed up—one had driven the 400-mile trip from Northern California and the other had driven almost 800 miles from El Paso to be there.

For this deployment, 2/1 had been part of a MEU, traveling on Navy ships. Since the ships returned as a group, unlike Daniel's homecoming, these Marines would all come home on the same day. This meant all the parents would be on the 2/1 parade grounds at the same time. I still maintained e-mail contact with the 2/1 parents, and I was excited to finally meet friends I had known only electronically for the past two years.

While the original plan was for the Marines to get into formation by companies on the parade grounds, many Marines were delayed because the off-loading of 2/1's weapons and vehicles from the ships took much longer than anticipated. The plan for a formal welcoming ceremony became defunct. Members of the various companies were straggling back from the ships in twos and threes. Some companies were being dismissed simultaneously in opposite corners of the field. The plan for Mario's presentation dissolved. Remember Semper Gumby? In all the chaos (including a sudden torrential downpour), Mario would have to just choose one company to which he could present the plaque. Naturally, he chose Fox Company. He congratulated the Marines, assured them of the love and admiration of the Vietnam vets, and thanked them for what they had done.

Very soon all the Marines were dismissed to the waiting arms of their loved ones. Some Marines were presented with new babies. Others brought their buddies over to meet members of their families. Some were parents of sons who would not be coming home, but wanted to meet their sons' friends. Since we didn't have a Marine coming home, we didn't have any of the underlying nervousness that accompanies homecoming. We were able to just drink in the moment and enjoy everyone's excitement.

We had a wonderful time; it felt like a satisfying resolution to the anxieties of our four-year military experience. One final moving incident was the perfect capstone to that homecoming.

I had been concerned that the morning's events on the parade deck might have been so disorganized that our two Vietnam vet friends might feel that it had not been worth their long drives to attend. When I asked them about it, one vet looked at me incredulously and said, "Oh, no! This has been wonderful! When I came home from Vietnam there was no ceremony and no one to greet me. I have been waiting for forty years for a homecoming. And today, watching these Marines come home, I feel as if I finally got it!"

Mario's experiences, as a 2/1 Marine in Vietnam, had once again intersected with Daniel's Marine experience with 2/1 in Iraq. The Marine Corps has shaped both father and son. The experiences of both Mario and Daniel have definitely sculpted our family dynamics. Though my husband was discharged from the Marine Corps several years before we even met, the residue of his war experience continues to be a lingering presence in our life together. When my son became a combat Marine, the Marine Corps again impacted my life at its most primordial level—fear for my child—and precipitated my reconsideration of values and beliefs. Who would have guessed that the Marine Corps, an institution in which I had never enlisted, would define *my* life so profoundly? Though the years my son was in the

Marine Corps and in Iraq were some of the worst in my life, they were also some of the best. The Marine Corps has changed me in many ways. Yet, I find that, rather than regret, my overarching feeling is one of gratitude for having been part of the Marine family. How true it is that we also serve.

Afterword

In the past several years, our lives have resumed a more predictable rhythm that is reassuring after the adrenalin-charged years of Daniel's time in the military. But, though my life has returned to a routine, it has been altered by those four years; they were some of the most significant—if not *the* most significant—of my life.

For all our worrying that Daniel did not want to come to Chico after Iraq, he has chosen to live in the same town. We see him frequently. He completed his inactive commitment in June 2008, for which my adrenal glands are grateful.

He has completed his undergraduate requirements and plans to begin upper division classes at California State University in Chico.

I admit that I continue to be observant of his moods should he exhibit behavior that suggests anger or depression issues. Despite having a lot of responsibilities, so far he seems to competently manage the varied and complex arenas of his life.

While in the Marine Corps, he had tired of the lonely bachelor life and was anxious to settle into a serious relationship and someday have a family.

Daniel is now married. His wife, Violeta, has two children, Genesis and Angel (from a previous marriage), whom we love having in our family. Together, Daniel and Violeta have three children. In an amazing turn of events, their son, Daniel Alejandro, was born on September 6, 2007—the same date as the Labor Day bombing three years before. Though Daniel was uncomfortable that his son was born on the same date that his friends had been killed, I feel altogether differently about it: for me, the birth offsets the painful events of that date. I was privileged to be present at the birth of Daniel's son, and, during that event, I felt the presence of those fallen Marines there with us. It was as if this baby was a gift from them, a nod to Daniel to go forward in his life with their blessing. To me, this baby is the miracle that so easily might not have been. Daniel and Violeta have since had a daughter Aminda (named for her great-grandmother) and a son John Paul.

More recently, our family has grown even more. All our sons have married and have blessed us with children of their own. In the fall of 2011, our daughter married Rich, a terrific man. We are very fortunate.

Forty years after his time in Vietnam, my husband finally filed a claim with the Veterans Administration for PTSD. More recently, to assist in obtaining an increased rating, not only did I write a letter detailing the effect of Mario's PTSD in our family, but our daughter Clarissa sent a note to the VA describing her perspective.

> ... I did not know until college that all dads did not have unbridled tempers and sudden outbursts of anger.... The sheer volume of anger was enough to make a room silent with fear. I honestly do not think there was a day in my childhood when my father did not lose his temper with us. Some symptoms I knew were a result of Vietnam. I remember [being in] our kitchen and accidentally slamming a cupboard door.... My father ducked to the ground. I had seen this reaction to loud noises before, but this time I caused it. Watching him duck to the ground was very difficult because he is usually so tough; yet, at that moment, I saw fear in his eyes. I still feel guilty for that moment.... There is no doubt in my mind war has made my dad a different person. He has paid a price that others will never know; he will always walk through life with a limp in his heart....

In November of 2007, Mario and I traveled to Houston to attend the yearly reunion of the Vietnam Veterans of 2nd Battalion 1st Marines. After several days of activities (including a Marine Corps birthday celebration), the Vietnam Veterans of 2/1 were the guests of honor at Houston's 2007 Veterans' Day parade. In a ceremony they were officially welcomed home by the city of Houston.

One of the 2/1 veterans, who helped to coordinate this event, informed us that he wanted the families—who, as he said, had earned their place in the Marine Corps family—to accompany the vets in the parade. Giddy with nervous anticipation on the morning of the parade, we began walking in phalanxes down the wide streets. Some veterans were able to fit into their original jungle utilities; the rest of us wore shirts with 2/1 insignia. We waved tiny American flags as onlookers cheered and waved back. When we walked past the reviewing stand, some young Marines in uniform rose to their feet, squared their shoulders, and saluted this group of older, paunchier, graying Marine vets. Touchingly, one very young combat-injured Marine, wearing dress blues and seated in a wheelchair, struggled to get up so he could stand at attention and salute as the vets passed by. Some bystanders carried signs bearing the words "Thank you, Vets." However, a middle-aged woman held the sign that choked me up. In red, white, and blue lettering, the poster proclaimed, "You are our heroes!" My heart melted with gratitude to that woman. For forty years Vietnam vets have been called many things, but when had they ever been called "heroes?"

The parade was pronounced by the veterans to be an unqualified success. In fact, they tittered with delight! After all these decades they had finally had a parade to honor *them*. Welcome home.

References

Below is a list of publications to which I referred while writing my book:

American Psychiatric Association, *Diagnostic and Statistical Manual of Mental Disorders, Fourth Edition*, Washington, DC, American Psychiatric Association Publishing, 2000.

Armstrong, Keith, LCSW, Best, Suzanne, PhD, and Domenici, Paula, PhD, *Courage After Fire*, Berkeley, California, Ulysses Press, 2006.

Aylworth, Roger H., "Brother Finds Himself Caught in the Middle," *Chico Enterprise-Record*, March 26, 2003, 1A+

Baker, Mark, *Nam*, New York, New York, William Morrow & Company, 1982.

Cantrell, Bridget C., Ph.D. and Dean, Chuck, *Down Range: To Iraq and Back*, Seattle, Washington, Word Smith Publishing, 2005.

Cantrell, Bridget C., Ph.D. and Dean, Chuck, *Once a Warrior: Wired for Life*, Seattle, Washington, Word Smith Publishing, 2007.

Henderson, Kristin, *While They're At War: The True Story of American Families on the Homefront*, New York, New York, Mariner Books, 2006.

Lanham, Stephanie Laite, *Veterans and Families' Guide to Recovering from PTSD*, Annandale Virginia, Purple Heart Foundation, 2005.

Matsakis, Aphrodite, Ph.D., *Vietnam Wives*, Baltimore, Maryland, The Sidran Press, 1996.

Pavlicin, Karen M., *Life After Deployment: Military Families Share Reunion Stories and Advice*, St. Paul, Minnesota, Elva Resa Publishing, 2007.

Simmons, Edwin Howard and Moskin, J. Robert, *The Marines*, New York, New York, Universe International Publications, 1998.

WEB SITES

Henderson, Kristin, *Anticipatory Grief*, 2006, reprinted on the author's Web site: http://www.kristinhenderson.com

www.marineparents.com: Information regarding the boot camp training matrix.

http://norfolkvisitor.com: Information about Norfolk Naval Station.

www.usmc.mil: General information about the Marine Corps.

RESOURCES

Additional resources are listed in many of the indices of the publications listed above, as well as in links on the Web sites below:

www.heartstowardhome.com Hearts Toward Home International is a non-profit organization founded by Dr. Bridget Cantrell. It provides information, counseling, education, and support for those military personnel who have returned from combat zones, as well as for their families, to enhance the reintegration of those troops in non-combat life after their deployment. The organization focuses particularly on those with PTSD.

www.joiningforces.gov Unveiled in April 2011, this national initiative, sponsored by Michelle Obama and Jill Biden, seeks to encourage all sectors of American society to offer concrete support to military families. This might take the form of employment or educational partnerships to personal supportive efforts by individuals.

www.kristinhenderson.com On this Web site there is a large bibliography of references and Web sites containing useful links for military spouses and families, addressing such topics as coping with deployment, accessing help, tips for the public regarding how to support the troops, resources for veterans, and a booklist of related reading material.

www.marineparents.com Founded by Tracy Della Vecchia in 2003, the Web site is a fount of information regarding all aspects of the Marine experience. I found the Web site's "recruitparents/bootcamp/trainingmatrix" link a particularly helpful reference regarding the boot camp training schedule. Much specific information about the training matrix in boot camp was obtained from the hyperlinks on this site. Just as importantly, the "message boards" are a vehicle of emotional support and allow family members of Marines the opportunity to meet and support each other across the miles.

www.militaryonesource.com Offers confidential, branch-specific, free assistance regarding post-combat, parenting, stress, relocation adjustment issues. This service is available to active duty, Guard, and Reserve personnel and their families twenty-four hours a day, seven days a week.

http://ncptsd.va.gov This Web site for the National Center for PTSD has a wealth of information for veterans and their families about PTSD, symptoms, treatments, where to find help, and more.

www.usmc.mil This is the official Marine Corps Web site, with information about careers, units, military life, as well as Marine Corps news.